Your Body Is Your Castle

a Six Week Guide To Eating Healthy and Weekly Meal Prepping

By Dr. Tandy Nance

ABOUT THE AUTHOR

As the Founder and CEO of Life Coach Tandy, LLC, Dr. Tandy Nance is a highly accomplished and dedicated Metaphysician, Certified Holistic Life Coach, Author, and Motivational Speaker. With over 18 years of experience in the mental health field, Dr. Tandy has amassed an impressive array of academic qualifications, including a bachelor's degree in criminal justice, master's degrees in counseling studies, master's degree in business administration, and a Doctorate in Metaphysical Humanistic Science.

In addition to her extensive education, Dr. Tandy is also a Certified Emotion and Body Code Energy Healing Practitioner and a Certified Clinical Hypnotherapist. Her wealth of knowledge and expertise allows her to provide her clients with a unique and comprehensive approach to healing and personal development.

Dr. Tandy is the author of "The Diva Code," the guide to leveling up, designed to encourage self improvement and the motivational self-help book "Boundaries + Clarity = Peace," which is designed to assist individuals who are struggling to create boundaries and gain the clarity necessary to make positive changes in their lives. Her books aim to empower people to find peace and fulfillment in their lives.

With a deep understanding of the mind, body, and spirit, Dr. Tandy's life purpose is to help others heal emotionally and move past traumatic events to fully achieve their desired life. She is passionate about empowering individuals to find their purpose and transform their lives beyond their wildest imagination. Through her unique combination of traditional and holistic techniques, Dr. Tandy is dedicated to helping her clients achieve true healing and lasting success.

Copyright Page

Dedication

This Book Is Dedicated to ME! And my journey and struggle to maintain a healthy eating process, healthy weight goals, and a positive body image. I will continue to be a work in progress. AND THAT'S OK!!!

Hey King & Queens

It's a struggle to stick to balanced eating habits. We all know that we should eat healthier. So why is it so hard? The bottom line is that eating healthy is not easy. Most of us would find calculus easier to do than creating healthy eating habits. But at the end of the day your body is your castle and you are kings and queens of your domain.

I know that eating is a behavior that is hard to understand. You need to eat to live, right! However, for most of us food is more than just something that provides sustenance, it's a part of our culture and sub subcultures. Think about it, we can't go any where or do anything without food being somewhere around.

This is what contributes to our eating habits, formed over years or decades. Some of these habits may be good, others you may be looking to change. And change is hard. But that's ok!!! I am always here for a challenge and transformation. All I ask is that you start taking small steps on your journey. Besides being given information on how to eat healthier, In this book you will be provided 6 weeks of recipes, grocery shopping lists, a 6 weeks meal plan, a mini food and mood journal. The journey begins now.

Dr. Tandy

PART 1

NUTRITION

What Is Nutrition?

Nutrients are the essential components we get from the foods we eat. These are components we should take in every day to guarantee the perfect functioning of the amazing castle that is our body. Just like calories, the need for nutrients varies greatly from person to person and the amount is determined by each person's needs.

Most of us pay little attention to nutrition and don't understand the basics of the building blocks of food. All foods are composed of calories from protein, carbohydrates, and fats. Water doesn't supply energy in the form of calories, but it is extremely vital to the castle.

To understand how what we eat affects the body, you will need to become familiar with the basics of nutrition:

Calories:
Calories are units of energy present in all food, including fats, proteins, and carbohydrates. Fats contain nine calories per gram, while carbohydrates and proteins contain four calories per gram.

Protein:
Proteins are the essential building blocks of life. Every cell in your body contains protein. These cells make up our skin, bones, muscle, organ issue and blood. Having the proper amounts of protein will prevent malnutrition, and the consumption of protein helps keep insulin from releasing from the body.

Fats:
Some dietary fats are more beneficial than others. Mono-unsaturated fats are "healthy" fats that are good for your heart and have a positive effect on blood cholesterol levels. Sources of healthy fats include olive oil, canola oil, and peanut oil. Polyunsaturated fats are needed in small amounts. Omega-3 fatty acids and Omega-6 fatty acids, found in fish, oils, and nuts are two types of polyunsaturated fats that are essential to your body. They are needed to make hormones and they also have a positive effect on blood cholesterol levels. "Unhealthy" saturated fats come from butter, lards, meat fats, full-fat dairy products, and coconut oil. These foods have a negative effect on blood cholesterol. Trans fats are another type of "unhealthy" fat that is found in some margarine, crackers, cookies, snack foods, and any processed food made with partially hydrogenated oils. Because fat has a high amount of calories, all fats need to be eaten in moderation.

Why Is Water Important To Your Health?
Water is key to all your body functions. Your body weight is 55-75% water. However, you lose water daily from perspiration, exhalation, urine, and feces. That's why it's essential to consume a minimum of 64 ounces of water daily to prevent dehydration. You need even more than this amount during hot summer months and during physical activity.

Your body cannot survive for more than five days without water, but dehydration sets in much faster. Caffeinated beverages such as coffee, tea, and alcoholic beverage can cause dehydration rapidly.

Nutritional Guidelines

So now that we got through the boring nutritional B.S. it's time to learn how to eat healthier. I'm going to give you five nutritional tips that are recommended by nutrition experts and backed up by scientific research. These are nutritional principles you can always count on during your journey to eating healthy and maintaining a healthy lifestyle, no matter what the fad is or no matter what is thrown your way follow these tips and you'll be ok .

1. Eat Plenty of Fruits and Vegetables

There are countless benefits to eating fruits and vegetables. They are loaded with vitamins and minerals, and are also filled with antioxidants, fiber, and lots of other beneficial ingredients. When you eat more fruits and veggies, you are more likely to eat fewer unhealthy foods.

2. Get Your Fiber

The American Heart Association recommends eating a total of 25 to 30 grams per day of fiber from food, not supplements. Fiber helps maintain a healthy digestive system, lower cholesterol, stabilize blood sugar, and keep weight in check. Fiber also helps you feel full, so you don't overeat.

3. Don't Forget To Hydrate

You need fluids to maintain every function in your body, including everyday duties performed by the heart, brain, and muscles. Fluids in your body also help carry nutrients to your cells and can also prevent constipation. Not to mention, dehydration can lead to unclear thinking, mood change, kidney stones, and cause the body to overheat, according to the CDC.

Women need approximately 9 cups of water and men need 12.5 cups of water per day, plus the water that comes from food. Besides plain water, you can get fluids from eating plenty of fruits and vegetables and other foods that naturally contain water.

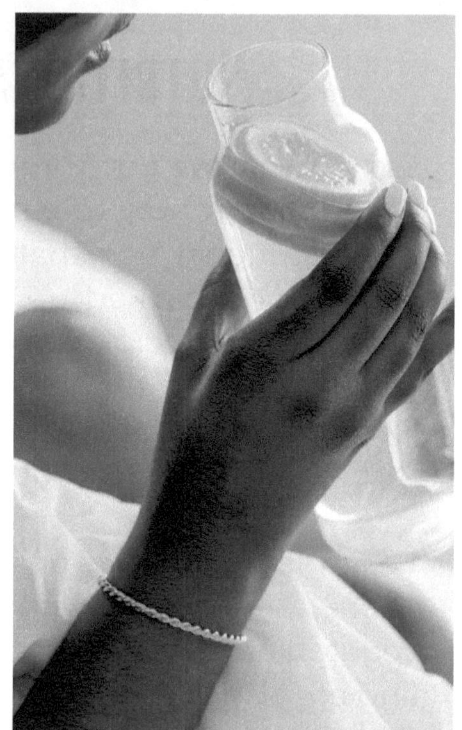

4. Have An Open Mind To Different Foods.

Your body needs a variety of nutrients in order to stay healthy. Be open to eating foods such as grains, nuts, seeds, fats, and more. The wider range of foods you eat in each of the various food groups, the greater variety of nutrients you'll take in. If you usually eat a salad with the same vegetables every day, maybe try switching it up. Instead of always choosing chicken, use seafood at least twice a week.

5. Limit Processed Foods

It's not breaking news that processed foods aren't good for the castle. But processed foods, in general, are not necessarily the issue. A bag of pre-washed salad greens, a slice of cheese, and a can of beans can all be considered processed, to a certain degree. It's the overly processed foods that provide few to no nutritional value. A good rule of thumb is to choose foods that are the closest to their original forms, such as fresh meat, chicken, fish, and fruits and vegetables for the most nutrients and the least added fat, sodium, and sugar.

We all love our cookies, donuts, and cakes. Start being mindful when you reach for the feel-good foods, because they are high in calories, saturated fat, and added sugar. Most of all they provide little to no vitamins and minerals. It's better to replace foods that are high in saturated fat with healthier options like apple or grapes.

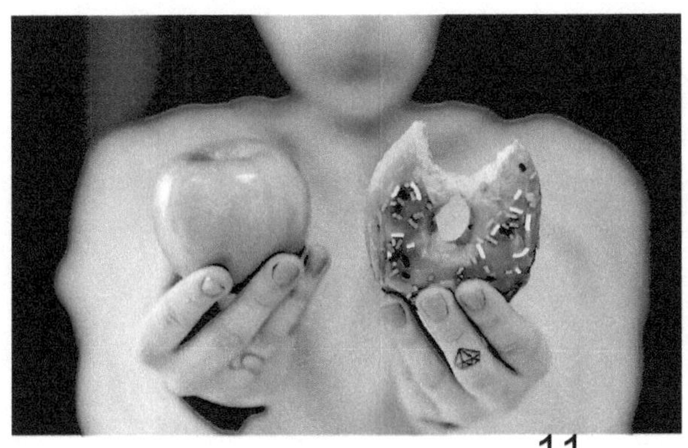

Understanding Nutritional Labels

Knowing more about the foods that you eat is one way to ensure healthy eating habits and maintain a healthy weight. The best way to know more about the food you eat is to read the nutrition label. Although it is required by the FDA that most foods have nutrition labels that include how much food is inside the package and what nutrients and ingredients are in the foods, reading the label can be a little confusing. When I first started my healthy eating journey over 20 years ago this was a process that was not as easy as it is today. The label was required for foods in the grocery store but not on foods in restaurants like they are today. Nevertheless, I was clueless to how important this was and was surprised to find out how high in calories and carbs many of my favorite foods were. So, here are some tips for reading and understanding a nutritional label...

1 Checking the serving size

The serving size is the first thing on the label. The size could be listed by cup, weight, or units. Under that you will see how many servings are in the package. Pay close attention and don't assume that the whole package is a single serving. For instance, a typical small bag of potato chips is probably two serving sizes.

Keep in mind the nutrition information on the label is for one serving, not the entire package. To get a total of calories and other nutrients for the entire package, multiply each of the numbers by the number of servings per container.

2 **What's the calories count?**

Next check out the calorie count. If you're trying to get to a healthy weight, you definitely want to take in fewer calories. Pay close attention to this number so you can understand how many calories you're consuming. Calories are important for getting to a healthy weight or maintaining a healthy weight. The meal plan is this book is designed to help you easily keep up with your daily calorie count.

3 **Look for the fat!**

You want to make sure the item doesn't have too much saturated fat, trans fats or sodium. There are two types of fats, saturated and trans fats. The AICR recommends limiting the amount of fat in your diet. A serving with 20% of the recommended daily value of fat is considered a high amount of fat, while 5% is considered low. The ACIR recommends limiting the amount of salt you eat to less than 2,400 milligrams a day. Salt is listed as sodium on a nutrition label. Try staying away from foods that have more than twice the milligrams of sodium than calories per serving.

4 **Pay attention to the carbohydrates.**

Carbohydrates should make up 45% to 65% of your total daily calories. Total carbohydrates are divided in to two categories on a label, dietary fiber, and sugar. Foods with fiber make you feel full and satisfied. This might help you lower your calorie intake and maintain a healthy weight. Foods with at least 3 grams of fiber per serving are considered a good source of fiber.

Small amounts of sugar can be a part of a healthy diet, but most of us consume too much. Eating too much sugar can lead to weight gain. Check the ingredients for items like, sugar, honey, corn syrup, fructose, maltose, dextrose, or cane syrup. These are other names for sugar sources in foods. It is recommended no more than six teaspoons of added sugar per day for women and nine teaspoons a day for men.

5 **Where are your proteins and vitamins?**
You want to make sure you're getting enough protein and vitamins. Dairy products, meat, and beans have protein. We need protein for our bodies to heal, grow, and function. It is recommended that we limit our red meats to about 18 ounces per week and again we should avoid processed meats. Many nutrition labels list vitamin A, vitamin C, calcium and iron. Most of us don't get enough of these vitamins. Look for foods high in these nutrients. It's better to get these nutrients by eating food rather than taking supplements.

Being aware of what to look for and how to read the nutrition label can help you make healthy choices. On the following page there is an example of a nutrition label. Get familiar with the label so that you are informed moving forward.

1 Check the serving size

2 Check the calories

3 Limit these!

4 Watch these

5 Get enough of these

Nutrition Facts

Serving Size 4 Cookies (32g)
Servings Per Container About 8

Amount Per Serving

Calories 160   Calories from Fat 70

% Daily Value*

Total Fat 8g	**12%**
Saturated Fat 5g	**25%**
Trans Fat 0g	
Polyunsaturated Fat 1g	
Monounsaturated Fat 1g	
Cholesterol 0mg	**0%**
Sodium 125mg	**5%**
Total Carbohydrate 22g	**7%**
Dietary Fiber less than 1g	**3%**
Sugars 10g	
Protein 1g	

Vitamin A 0%	•	Vitamin C 0%
Calcium 0%	•	Iron 4%

*Percent Daily Values are based on a 2,000 calorie diet. Your daily values may be higher or lower depending on your calorie needs:

		Calories:	2,000	2,500
Total Fat	Less than		65g	80g
Sat Fat	Less than		20g	25g
Cholesterol	Less than		300mg	300mg
Sodium	Less than		2,400mg	2,400mg
Total Carbohydrate			300g	375g
Dietary Fiber			25g	30g

Now let's practice making healthy choices...

Examine the following nutrition labels and answer the questions.

1. How many calories would you take in if you ate the whole box of crackers in one sitting? _______________________

2. If you ate 2 servings of crackers, how many grams of carbohydrates would you get? _______________________

3. If each gram of carbohydrates provides 4 calories, how many calories would you take in by eating 2 servings of crackers? _______________________

4. If fat provides 9 calories per gram, how many calories would you get by eating 2 servings? _______________________

Nutrition Facts

Serving Size 2 crackers (14 g)
Servings Per Container About 21

Amount Per Serving

Calories 60   Calories from Fat 15

	% Daily Value*
Total Fat 1.5g	2%
Saturated Fat 0g	0%
Trans Fat 0g	
Cholesterol 0mg	0%
Sodium 70mg	3%
Total Carbohydrate 10g	3%
Dietary Fiber Less than 1g	3%
Sugars 0g	
Protein 2g	

Vitamin A 0%	•	Vitamin C 0%
Calcium 0%	•	Iron 2%

* Percent Daily Values are based on a 2,000 calorie diet. Your daily values may be higher or lower depending on your calorie needs:

		Calories:	2,000	2,500
Total Fat	Less than		65g	80g
Sat Fat	Less than		20g	25g
Cholesterol	Less than		300mg	300mg
Sodium	Less than		2400mg	2400mg
Total Carbohydrate			300g	375g
Dietary Fiber			25g	30g

Chicken Noodle Soup

Nutrition Facts

Serving Size 1/2 cup (120 ml) condensed soup
Servings Per Container about 2.5

Amount Per Serving

Calories 60	Calories from Fat 15
	% Daily Value*
Total Fat 1.5g	2%
Saturated Fat 0.5g	3%
Trans Fat 0g	
Cholesterol 15mg	
Sodium 890gm	37%
Total Carbohydrate 8g	3%
Dietary Fiber 1g	4%
Sugars 1g	
Protein 3g	

Vitamin A	4%	Calcium	0%
Vitamin C	0%	Iron	2%

*Percent Daily Values are based on a 2,000 calorie diet. Your Daily Values may be higher or lower depending on your calorie needs.

		Calories	2000	2500
Total Fat	Less than		65g	80g
Sat Fat	Less than		20g	25g
Cholesterol	Less than		300mg	300mg
Sodium	Less than		2,400mg	2400mg
Total Carbohydrate			300g	375g
Dietary Fiber			25g	30g

5. If you were to eat the entire can of soup, how much sodium would you consume? _______________________

6. If the recommended amount of sodium for someone with high blood pressure is 1500 mg/ day, how much more than the recommended amount is present in this entire can?

____

7. How many servings of soup would I need to consume 20% of my daily requirement of fiber? _______________________

8. How many calories would that be? _______________________

Ingredients: Whole Corn, Vegetable Oil (Contains One or More of the Following: Corn, Soybean, and/or Sunflower Oil), Salt, Cheddar Cheese (Cultured Milk, Salt, Enzymes), Maltodextrin, Wheat Flour, Whey, Monosodium Glutamate, Buttermilk Solids, Romano Cheese from Cow's Milk (Part-Skim Cow's Milk, Cheese Cultures, Salt, Enzymes), Whey Protein Concentrate, Onion Powder, Partially Hydrogenated Soybean and Cottonseed Oil, Corn Flour, Disodium Phosphate, Lactose, Natural and Artificial Flavor, Dextrose, Tomato Powder, Spices, Lactic Acid, Artificial Color (Including Yellow 6, Yellow 5, Red 40), Citric Acid, Sugar, Garlic Powder, Red and Green Bell Pepper Powder, Sodium Caseinate, Disodium Inosinate, Disodium Guanylate, Nonfat Milk Solids, Whey Protein Isolate, and Corn Syrup Solids.
CONTAINS MILK AND WHEAT INGREDIENTS.

Nutrition Facts

Serving Size 1

Amount Per Serving

Calories 140	Calories from Fat 70

	% Daily Value*
Total Fat 8g	**12%**
Saturated Fat 1.5g	**7%**
Trans Fat 0g	
Cholesterol 0mg	**0%**
Sodium 160mg	**7%**
Total Carbohydrate 17g	**6%**
Dietary Fiber 1g	**6%**
Sugars 1g	
Protein 2g	

Vitamin A 0%	•	Vitamin C 0%
Calcium 2%	•	Iron 2%
Vitamin E 4%	•	Thiamin 4%
Vitamin B6 4%	•	Phosphorus 6%

* Percent Daily Values are based on a 2,000 calorie diet. Your daily values may be higher or lower depending on your calorie needs:

		Calories:	2,000	2,500
Total Fat	Less than		65g	80g
Sat Fat	Less than		20g	25g
Cholesterol	Less than		300mg	300mg
Sodium	Less than		2,400mg	2,400mg
Total Carbohydrate			300g	375g
Dietary Fiber			25g	30g

Calories per gram:
Fat 9 • Carbohydrate 4 • Protein 4

*** This serving size is 1 ounce. An average bag of Doritos contains 16 ounces of chips, for a total of 16 servings per bag.***

9. How many calories would you consume if you ate the whole 16oz bag? _______________

10. How many carbohydrates would you consume if you ate the whole bag? _______________

11. What percentage is this of your daily intake of carbohydrates?

____

12. How much fat would you get from eating 5 servings of Doritos?

____

13. How much saturated fat would you get if you ate the whole bag?

____

Assume the same sized bag – 16 servings per bag...

14. How much saturated fat would you get from eating the whole bag of Baked Doritos?

____

15. How many carbohydrates would you get if you ate the entire bag?

____

16. How much less fat would there be in eating an entire bag of Baked vs. Regular chips? _______________

18. What major nutrient increases per serving when comparing Baked vs. Regular chips?

____

Ingredients: Whole Corn, Corn Oil, Salt, Cheddar Cheese (Milk, Cheese Cultures, Salt, Enzymes), Buttermilk Solids, Whey Protein Concentrate, Whey, Tomato Powder, Monosodium Glutamate, Romano Cheese (Part Skim Cow's Milk, Cheese Cultures, Salt, Enzymes), Onion Powder, Wheat Flour, Natural and Artificial Flavor, Partially Hydrogenated Soybean and Cottonseed Oil, Artificial Color (Including Yellow 6 Lake, Yellow 5 Lake, Yellow 6, Red 40 Lake), Sugar, Garlic Powder, Disodium Phosphate, Dextrose, Parmesan Cheese (Part-Skim Milk, Cheese Cultures, Salt, Enzymes), Spice, Citric Acid, Lactic Acid, Disodium Inosinate, and Disodium Guanylate.
CONTAINS MILK AND WHEAT INGREDIENTS.

Nutrition Facts

Serving Size 1 oz.

Amount Per Serving

Calories 120	Calories from Fat 30

	% Daily Value*
Total Fat 3.5g	**6%**
Saturated Fat 0.5g	**3%**
Polyunsaturated Fat 2g	
Monounsaturated Fat 1g	
Trans Fat 0g	
Cholesterol 0mg	**0%**
Sodium 220mg	**9%**
Total Carbohydrate 21g	**7%**
Dietary Fiber 2g	**7%**
Sugars 1g	
Protein 2g	

Vitamin A 2%	•	Vitamin C 0%
Calcium 4%	•	Iron 2%
Vitamin E 2%	•	Thiamin 4%
Niacin 2%	•	Vitamin B6 6%
Phosphorus 6%	•	Zinc 2%

* Percent Daily Values are based on a 2,000 calorie diet. Your daily values may be higher or lower depending on your calorie needs:

		Calories:	2,000	2,500
Total Fat	Less than		65g	60g
Sat Fat	Less than		20g	25g
Cholesterol	Less than		300mg	300mg
Sodium	Less than		2,400mg	2,400mg
Total Carbohydrate			300g	375g
Dietary Fiber			25g	30g

Calories per gram:
Fat 9 • Carbohydrate 4 • Protein 4

"you cant control everything, but you can control what you put in your body."

Recipe's

Trying new recipes can be fun! And it's usually easier to stay healthy with a home-cooked meal versus going out. No matter what recipe you are looking to try, if it isn't in the context of your healthy eating plan, it defeats the purpose. When looking for healthy recipes, think about what you have eaten that day, or what you plan to eat the rest of the day or week. For example, if you haven't eaten veggies all day, consider making a meal with mostly vegetables.

Cooking healthy can be a challenge for many reasons. Part of the struggle is finding good recipes that are easy to fix and fit into a healthy meal plan. Whether you need low carb, sugar free, or low calories. I've put together eight of my favorite healthy recipes.

SHRIMP TACO BOWLS

PREP TIME 10 MINUTES
COOK TIME 15 MINUTES
TOTAL TIME 25 MINUTES
SERVINGS 4
CALORIES 335KCAL

INGREDIENTS
SPICY SHRIMP:
20 MEDIUM SHRIMP PEELED AND DEVEINED
1 TABLESPOON OLIVE OIL
1 CLOVE GARLIC MINCED
1/2 TEASPOON GROUND CUMIN
1/2 TEASPOON CHILI POWDER
1/4 TEASPOON ONION POWDER OPTIONAL
1/4 TEASPOON KOSHER SALT
FOR THE ASSEMBLY:
2 CUPS COOKED BROWN RICE
1 CUP BLACK BEANS DRAINED AND RINSED
1 CUP CORN DRAINED AND RINSED
1 CUP TOMATOES DICED
1/2 CUP CHEDDAR CHEESE
2 TABLESPOON CILANTRO MINCED
1 LIME CUT INTO 4 SLICES
4 MEAL PREP CONTAINERS

Instructions

1.	To cook the shrimp: In a medium bowl whisk together olive oil, garlic, cumin, chili and onion powders, and salt. Add in shrimp and toss to coat completely. Cover and refrigerate for for at least 10 minutes or up to 24 hours. Heat a large heavy-duty or cast iron skillet on high heat for 2 minutes. Add the olive oil and shrimp. Cook shrimp in a skillet on medium-high heat until pink and cooked through, about 5 minutes.

2.	To assemble: Divide brown rice into 4 meal prep containers (1/2 cup each). Top with 5 shrimps, a scoop of black beans, corn, tomatoes, a sprinkle of cheese, cilantro and a slice of lime. Cover and refrigerate for a max of 4 days.

3.	To serve: Heat bowls in the microwave for 2 minutes or until heated thoroughly. Drizzle with lime juice and top with salsa, sour-cream or guacamole if desired.

Notes

Cook brown rice according to package directions before getting started on the shrimp so it cooks while you are preparing the shrimp.l bites. We added a few extra toppings to make it a bite full of flavor.

CHICKEN AND BROCCOLI STIR FRY

SERVINGS: 8
PREP TIME: 15 MINUTES
COOK TIME: 10 MINUTES
TOTAL TIME: 25 MINUTES

INGREDIENTS
2 TBSP OLIVE OIL
2 GARLIC CLOVES MINCED
2 LBS CHICKEN BREAST THINLY SLICED
8 CUPS BROCCOLI FLORETS
4 CARROTS PEELED AND THINLY SLICED
4 SCALLIONS THINLY SLICED
4 CUPS OF COOKED BROWN RICE

FOR THE STIR FRY SAUCE
4 TBSP OYSTER SAUCE
2 TSP LOW SODIUM SOY SAUCE
2 TBSP SESAME OIL
2 TSP FRESHLY GRATED GINGER
2 TSP SRIRACHA SAUCE
3 TSP CORNSTARCH

Instructions

1.   For this recipe you will need a very large wok or skillet, or you can make it in two batches, otherwise your ingredients will not all fit. In a small bowl, add all the stir fry sauce ingredients and whisk together.

2.   Add oil and garlic to your pan and bring to medium high heat. Once oil is heated, add in chicken and cook until chicken is about 2/3 done.

3.   Add in the broccoli and carrots and cook until everything is just cooked. Pour in about half of the stir fry sauce and stir it evenly into the broccoli, carrots and chicken. Taste and add more sauce as needed. You may not want to add the entire sauce amount. I used about 2/3 of the sauce in total. If you prefer a thicker sauce, you can add more cornstarch into your stir fry to thicken the sauce. Once everything is cooked and evenly coated in sauce, turn off heat. Sprinkle scallions over stir fry.

4.   Add 1/2 cup of brown rice to each of your meal prep containers. Divide your stir fry into about 8 equal portions and add to the containers. Store in fridge and consume within 3-4 days.

BANANA PANCAKES

SERVINGS: 2
PREP TIME: 10 MINUTES
COOK TIME: 10 MINUTES
TOTAL TIME: 20 MINUTES

INGREDIENTS
FOR 4 SERVINGS
2 RIPE BANANAS
2 EGGS
1 TEASPOON VANILLA EXTRACT
½ CUP QUICK-COOK OATS
1 TEASPOON CINNAMON

Instructions

Mash bananas in a large bowl until smooth. Mix in eggs and vanilla until well combined, then mix in oats and cinnamon. Heat a skillet to medium and add in a scoop* of the pancake batter. Smooth out to form an even layer. Cook for about 2-3 minutes until you start to see bubbles releasing from the top of the batter. Flip and cook until the other side is golden brown, about 1-2 minutes.

Garnish your pancakes with your favorite toppings! We used banana slices, chopped walnuts & maple syrup.

*Note: Use ½ cup (65) for scooping the batter to yield 4 thicker pancakes; Use ⅓ cup (40 g) to yield 6 smaller pancakes.

Enjoy!

TACO SOUP

SERVINGS: 6
PREP TIME: 10 MINUTES
COOK TIME: 6 HOURS

INGREDIENTS
FOR 4 SERVINGS
3 BONELESS CHICKEN BREAST
1PACKET OF TACO SAUCE
1 MEDIUM ONION
1 CAN 14.5 OZ. ROTEL
TOMATOES W/GREEN CHILIES
1 CAN BLACK BEANS
1 CANNELLINI OR PINTO
BEANS
1 CAN KIDNEY BEANS
1 CAN WHOLE KERNEL CORN
1 CAN 8 OZ. TOMATO SAUCE

Instructions
Put everything into a crockpot in the order listed. Do not rinse or drain beans. DO NOT STIR!
Cook on low for 6-8 hours. Take chicken out and shred with fork. Put chicken back in . Stir and eat.

SRIRACHA CAULIFLOWER FRIED RICE

SERVINGS: 4
PREP TIME: 10 MINUTES
COOK TIME: 15 MINUTES
TOTAL TIME: 25 MINUTES

INGREDIENTS
2 TBSP OLIVE OIL
1 LB CHICKEN BREAST CUT INTO BITE-
SIZED CUBES
6 CUPS OF CAULIFLOWER RICE (SEE NOTE)
1 RED BELL PEPPER CUT INTO 1/2 INCH
SQUARES
1 CUP CUT (1-INCH LONG) GREEN
BEANS·
2-3 TBSP LOW SODIUM SOY SAUCE
1 TBSP SESAME OIL
2 TSP SRIRACHA SAUCE   SALT AND
PEPPER TO TASTE
1 GREEN SCALLION FINELY SLICED

Instructions
Instructions

1. In a large skillet or pan, add 1 tbsp olive oil and bring to medium heat. Add in chicken and cook until chicken is just cooked. I like to turn the heat slightly higher and give the chicken a seared exterior before turning the heat back down again.

2. Add in remaining olive oil. Add in cauliflower rice, bell pepper and green beans. Stir and cook until vegetables are halfway cooked. Add in soy sauce, sesame oil and sriracha. Stir until completely mixed and vegetables are tender but still crisp. Taste and adjust seasoning as needed. Stir in scallions for a few seconds before turning off heat.

3. Dish out into meal prep containers. Allow rice to cool before refrigerating or freezing. If desired, you can add a drizzle of sriracha sauce on top of rice. Reheat before eating.

4-INGREDIENT FREEZER BREAKFAST BURRITOS

SERVINGS: 8
PREP TIME: 30 MINS
TOTAL TIME: 30 MINS

INGREDIENTS
1 LB. BREAKFAST
98 % FAT FREE GROUND
TURKEY OR CHICKEN
12 EGGS
SALT AND PEPPER TO
TASTE
8 THIN SLICES OF FAT
FREE CHEDDAR CHEESE
8 OLE WRAPS SLICED

Instructions

Breakfast Sausage Mixture:

1.   Heat a large skillet over medium heat. Add breakfast sausage. Cook until meat is no longer pink. Stir frequently. Remove from heat and set aside.

Scrambled Eggs:

1.   Beat eggs, salt and pepper in a medium bowl until blended.

2.   Lightly coat a large nonstick skillet with olive oil spray. Pour in egg mixture. As eggs begin to set, gently pull the eggs across the pan with a spatula forming curds.

3.   Continue cooking – pulling, lifting and folding eggs – until thickened and no visible liquid egg remains. Don't stir constantly. Remove from heat. Set aside.

Assembly:

1.   Place 1 slice of cheese in the center of each tortilla. Add about 1/12 of the eggs and 1/12 of the sausage to the tortilla. Fold the sides into the center of the tortilla and then roll into a burrito. Burritos can be individually wrapped in parchment paper (if you plan to heat in microwave) or aluminum foil (if you plan to heat in the oven) and placed into an airtight zipper bag and placed in the freezer.

To Heat Burritos:

·   Oven: Bake breakfast burritos (foil and all) in an oven that has been heated to 425 degrees for 45 minutes. Halfway through the cooking process, flip the burritos so that they cook evenly.

·   Microwave: Remove the foil from the burrito and microwave for about 90 seconds (cooking time will vary depending on the size of your burrito). Allow the burrito to cool before enjoying.

Notes

You can also heat the burritos in the oven at 350 degrees right after you assemble them and serve immediately. I do like to freeze the leftovers because the burritos can become soggy if stored in the refrigerator.

TACO BOWLS WITH CAULIFLOWER RICE

SERVINGS: 4
PREP TIME: 20 MINUTES
COOK TIME: 10 MINUTES
TOTAL TIME: 30 MINUTES

INGREDIENTS
1 CLOVE GARLIC MINCED
1/2 SMALL BROWN ONION PEELED AND FINELY CHOPPED
1 TBSP OLIVE OIL
1 LB LEAN GROUND TURKEY
1 PACKET LIGHT TACO SEASONING OR THE HOMEMADE TACO SEASONING BELOW
1 (15-OZ) CAN BLACK BEANS RINSED AND DRAINED
1 (15.25-OZ) CAN WHOLE KERNEL CORN DRAINED
2 LARGE TOMATOES DICED
1 LARGE AVOCADO CUBED
1/2 CUP FAT FREE SHREDDED CHEDDAR CHEESE
FRESH CILANTRO FOR GARNISH
1 PACKAGE OF TACO SEASON

Instructions

1. In a large skillet add garlic, onion and oil. Bring pan to medium high heat. Stir and cook until onions are halfway done and aroma of the garlic has been released. Add in ground turkey and cook until browned. Add in taco seasoning packet and water amount specified in instructions. If using the homemade taco seasoning, start with 1 tbsp+ 1/4 cup water and add more as needed. I ended up using 2 tbsp and 1/2 cup water. Stir the seasoning into the ground turkey mixture and cook until turkey is completely cooked. Drain any excess fat. (If you are using very lean ground turkey, you may not have any excess fat.)

2. In a separate skillet, prepare the cauliflower rice. Add in oil and bring to medium high heat. Add in cauliflower rice and season with salt and pepper as needed. Cook until cauliflower is tender.

3. When rice and turkey have cooled, you can package into your meal prep containers. First, divide the cauliflower rice evenly across four containers. Add ground turkey to one side of each of the containers. Then add rows of corn, black beans and tomatoes. You can also add avocado now or you can wait until day of eating if you don't want your avocado to brown. Sprinkle cheese across or add as another row. Garnish with cilantro. You can also add lime wedges to squeeze on right before eating.*

TEX-MEX CHICKEN MEAL PREP BOWLS

SERVINGS: 4
PREP TIME: 15 MINS
COOK TIME: 20 MINS
TOTAL TIME: 35 MINS

INGREDIENTS

1 CUP UNCOOKED BROWN   2 CUPS LOW-SODIUM CHICKEN BROTH
3 TABLESPOONS OLIVE OIL 1 POUND BONELESS SKINLESS CHICKEN BREAST, CUT
INTO SMALL BITE-SIZE PIECES
2 TEASPOONS TACO SEASONING MIX
2 BELL PEPPERS ANY COLOR, SLICED INTO THIN STRIPS
1/2 SMALL WHITE OR YELLOW ONION THINLY SLICE
2 TEASPOONS MINCED GARLIC
1 SMALL ZUCCHINI CHOPPED
1 CUP FROZEN CORN
SALT AND FRESH GROUND BLACK PEPPER TO TASTE
2 TABLESPOONS CHOPPED FRESH CILANTRO OPTIONAL   1 15 OUNCE CAN
BLACK BEANS, RINSED AND DRAINED WELL FRESH LIME WEDGES

Instructions

1.   Cook rice according to package directions, substituting chicken broth for the water, if desired.

2.   Meanwhile, add 2 tablespoons olive oil to a saute pan and place over MEDIUM heat. Add chicken pieces and season with taco seasoning. Cook, stirring, until chicken is completely cooked through. Remove from heat and transfer chicken to a plate to cool.

3.   Add remaining olive oil to the same pan and return to MEDIUM heat. Add bell peppers and onion. Cook and stir until bell pepper is slightly softened, about 2 or 3 minutes. Add garlic, zucchini and frozen corn. Cook and stir until zucchini is crisp tender, an additional 2 or 3 minutes. Season veggies with a touch of salt and fresh ground pepper while cooking. Remove from heat and set aside.

4.   Divide the cooked rice among the 4 meal prep containers. Sprinkle cilantro over rice (if desired). Add an even amount of the cooked chicken, cooked veggies, and black beans on top of the rice in the containers. Add a lime wedge and a topping container filled with your topping of choice.

Cover and store in refrigerator. When ready to eat, reheat uncovered container in microwave for 1-1/2 to 2 minutes just until warm. Squeeze with lime juice and top with sour cream, salsa, or dressing of your choice.

PART 2

WHY HEALTHY FOODS

Eating Healthy Is a Form Of Self Respect

Food is often used as a motivator, a treat, or a reward. When our children have good behavior as babies, we treat the good behavior with a snack. In almost every culture food is used as a motivator for parties, holidays, and every family function. If food wasn't involved 9 times out of 10 you wouldn't even show up. As a matter a fact when you're invited to a gathering the first thing you probably ask is "What's on the menu?" and the second question is "Who's cooking?"

So how do we figure out how to eat healthy and be the healthiest versions of ourselves, while still living a life that doesn't feel restricted? It's complicated, that's why I wrote a book about it! But think of it this way, when you respect yourself and your body, you think twice about what you put in the castle. This is not me recommending any form of restriction or a dieting mindset. Its counterproductive to withhold or deprive yourself of the foods that you enjoy. When self- respect is the disposition making food choices becomes a matter of empowerment moving you from a diet mindset, "I can't have that" to a empowering mindset, "I choose not to have that". And so far, I have given you some useful tips (and there are more to come) to help you make the best choice possible on deciding what to eat.

But when it relates to thinking of this process as a degree of self-respect. There are a series of questions to ask yourself when choosing foods to eat especially when it's not the everyday circumstances (i.e., parties, holidays, events). Before eating, ask your food: "What do you have to offer me?" Ideally the answer should be nutrients (i.e., fiber, protein, healthy fat etc.)

If it's not for nutrients you want to ask your food, "Are you worth it and enjoyable to eat?" This question is extremely important! If the food does not offer any forms of nutrition it should offer some form of pleasure, otherwise at the end of the meal you might feel disappointed and dissatisfied. Have you ever had a meal that felt unsatisfying, and you end up mindlessly look around for other foods that would give you the sense of pleasure you didn't get from the unenjoyable meal? To avoid this, make sure the food choice is worth it!

The next big question is to ask yourself "Self, am I actually hungry for this food?" If you get the answer yes, eat the food! If the answer is no, ask yourself "Self, do I want to eat this for any reason other than it is tasty or fueling my body?" If you get a yes, ask yourself "Self, why do I want to eat this food?"This is the part of the question game that might get interesting. If eating the food is for comfort, avoiding eventful emotions, or to fill any other void in your life, this would be considered emotional eating.

Emotional Eating

Sometimes food serves as more than a nutritional purpose. We don't always eat to satisfy hunger pains. More times than often we go to food for comfort, stress relief, or to reward ourselves. And when this happens, we want junk food, sweets, and other comfort foods. I had a friend that would drink a whole liter of Dr. Pepper when she was feeling down or stressed out. When I was younger boredom would drive me to my salty comfort foods.

Emotional eating is when you use food to make yourself feel better, to fill emotional needs, rather than fueling your body. Unfortunately, emotional eating doesn't fix emotional problems. In fact, in my past experiences it usually made me feel worse. After I stuffed my face with comfort foods, not only did the original issue remain present, but I felt guilty for eating unhealthily.

If you want to know if you are an emotional eater. Ask yourself the following questions....

Do I eat more when I feel stressed?

Do I eat to feel better (to calm and soothe yourself when you're sad, mad, bored, anxious, etc.)?

Does food make me feel safe? Do I feel like food is my friend?

Do I feel powerless or out of control around food?

If you answered yes to most of these questions it's ok. Hell, I answered yes to most of them! In order to address emotional eating, it's important to understand the cycle and know the difference between emotional hunger and physical hunger.

The Emotional Eating Cycle.

Using food as a means to feel better, to celebrate, or reward yourself isn't always a bad thing. It's a problem when it turns into a coping mechanism. When your first reaction to stress, being upset, angry, lonely, tired, or bored is to go to the refrigerator can get you stuck in an unhealthy cycle where true emotions or problems are never addressed.

When you combine the issues, you can't learn healthier ways to deal with your emotions, it'll be difficult to maintain a healthy weight, and you begin to feel powerless over both food and your emotions. But no matter how powerless you start to feel over your food choices and your emotions, I'm here to tell you it is possible to change these habits. You can learn healthier ways to deal with your emotions, avoid your triggers, and finally put a stop to emotional eating.

The Emotional Eating Cycle

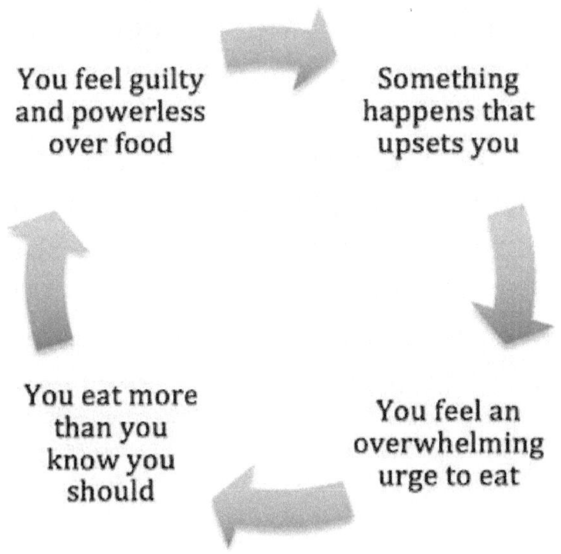

Emotional Hunger vs. Physical Hunger

Before you can break the cycle of emotional eating, you first need to learn the difference between emotional and physical hunger. This might be harder than it sounds, especially if your usual is to go to your comfort foods to fill voids or mask your emotions.

Emotional hunger can be powerful and it's very easy to mistake it for physical hunger. But I'm going to give you 5 ways you can distinguish between being physically hungry and emotional hungry.

1.   Emotional hunger comes suddenly. It hits you in an instant and feels overwhelming and urgent. Physical hunger, on the other hand, comes on more gradually. The urge to eat doesn't feel as dire unless you haven't eaten for a very long time.

2.   Emotional hunger isn't satisfied once you're full. You keep wanting more usually until you're stuffed and uncomfortable. Physical hunger doesn't need to be stuffed. You feel satisfied when your stomach is full.

3.   Emotional hunger craves certain comfort foods. When you're physically hungry, almost anything sounds good, including healthy stuff like vegetables. But emotional hunger craves junk food or sugary snacks that provide an instant rush. My friend who drank Dr. Pepper when she was stressed is a good example.

4.   Emotional hunger often leads to mindless eating. Before you know it, you've eaten a whole package of Oreo's. When you eat because your physically hungry, you typically have more awareness.

5.   Emotional hunger often leads to regret, guilt, or shame. When you eat to satisfy physical hunger, you're unlikely to feel guilty or ashamed because you've fueled your body with what it needs. If you feel guilty after you eat, it's most likely because you know you were not really hungry.

Know Your Triggers

If you want to stop emotional eating, you must become aware of your triggers. What situations, places, or feelings make you want to go to your comfort foods? Emotional eating is not only linked to stressful experience or feelings, but it can also be triggered by positive emotions, such as rewarding yourself for achieving a goal or celebrating a holiday or happy event.

Note if...

Stress makes you hungry. That's not your imagination. When stressed your body produces high levels of the stress hormone, cortisol. Cortisol triggers cravings for salty, sweet, and fried foods. If you are stressed, you are more likely to turn to foods for emotional relief.

You are suppressing your emotions, such as anger, fear, sadness, anxiety, loneliness, resentment, and shame. Numbing yourself with food could be your way of avoiding the difficult emotions you'd rather not feel.

You are feeling bored or empty. Do you ever eat because you have nothing else better to do or as a way to fill a void in your life? When you feel unfulfilled and empty food could be a way to occupy your mouth and your time. At that moment, you feel fulfilled, and your being distracted from the real issue which is purposelessness and dissatisfaction with your life.

You are repeating childhood behaviors. Did your parents reward good behavior with the "fun foods" or when you were feeling sad, they gave you "comfort foods'? This is a habit that could have carried over to adulthood.

Finding Other ways to Cope.

If you can't manage your emotions in a way that doesn't involve food, you will not be able to manage your eating habits. To stop emotional eating, you must find other ways to fulfill yourself emotionally. Understand the cycle of emotional eating or knowing your triggers is a good start, but it's not enough! You also need to find other things that you can go to for emotional fulfillment.

One of the best ways to identify the patterns behind your emotional eating is to keep track with a food and mood journal. Everyone who knows me, knows my thought process on journaling. Journaling allows for a level of self-awareness that may not be present through your conscious mind. So, when you are triggered to reach for your comfort food, stop and take a moment to figure out what triggered the urge. Write it all down in your food and mood journal: what you ate (or wanted to eat), what triggered you, how you felt and what you were thinking before you ate, what you felt and what you were thinking as you were eating, and how you felt and thoughts afterwards.

My personal favorite is to use energy healing. If you have read my previous books or worked with me before you know that I am certified in Emotion and Body Code which is an energy healing modality. Delete a food is a technique that I have used through emotion code for myself and for my clients to remove all trapped emotions that are causing you to crave or eat a food or drink that you would like to stop consuming but are unable to do so. If you want to learn more about energy healing or the delete a food technique, go to www.mylifecoachtandy.com and book a 15 min discover call.

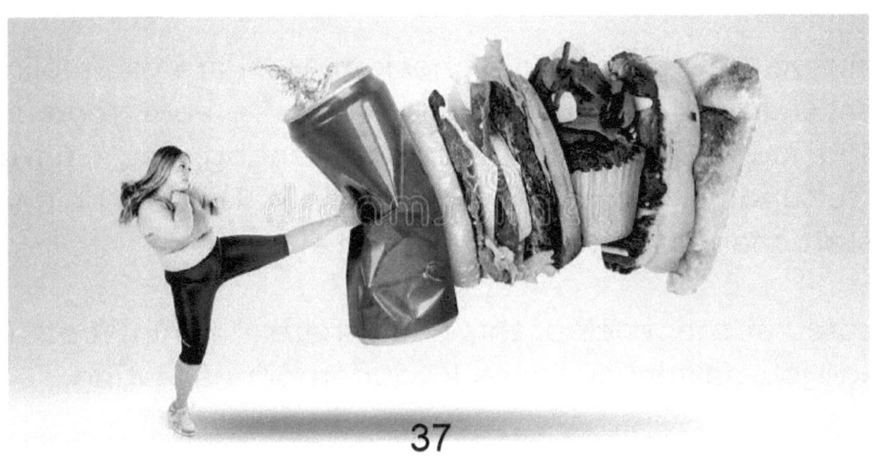

Also here are some other quick tips if you are feeling...

Depressed or lonely: Call someone who always makes you laugh. For me that's my best friend. We laugh at the craziest things even when we probably shouldn't.

Anxious: Release nervous energy by dancing to your favorite song. Energy healing is also a good method to address anxiety.

Drained; Take a healing bath, light some scented candles, or listen to high frequency or sound bath music.

Bored: Watch a good movie, watch a comedy show, explore the outdoors, or do an activity you enjoy.

Your emotional eating could be set on auto polite and before you even realized it you've reached for your favorite comfort food. But if you take a second to reflect on what is going on, you give yourself the opportunity to make a different decision.

Try a 5 min pause. Don't fight against the craving; remember, resisting the craving actually causes you to crave it more. Just tell yourself to wait.

While you're waiting, do a check in. How are you feeling? What's going on emotionally? Write in your food and mood journal, even if you end up eating, you'll have a better understanding of why you did it. This will help you to start changing the behavior in the future.

Located at the back of this book there is a mini food and mood journal for you to track your emotional eating.

Choosing Healthy Foods

Choosing to eat healthy is the first step towards a healthy lifestyle. I know that choosing the right foods can be confusing. But remember, foods that you eat act as a fuel, that keeps your body and mind running properly.

There are many reasons why you should choose healthy foods over unhealthy foods. The main reason why your food choices matter is because food can have a dramatic impact on your overall health and well-being. By choosing healthy foods, you can avoid a number of health problems. For instance, people who eat lots of fruits and vegetables have less problems with being overweight and are less likely to contract a cold or the. flu.

Healthy food choices also promote healthy weight. As I stated earlier processed foods and sweets are loaded with calories, healthy foods are typically low in calorie and high in essential nutrients. It's not just our physical health that is affected by healthy eating. Research has shown that healthy eating can have a positive impact on mental health. Healthy foods rich in vitamins and minerals are associated with lowering the risk for mental health disorders such as anxiety and depression.

~ Top 80 Health Foods ~

Start Eating Healthy Today!

Veggies

Asparagus
Carrots
Celery
Kale
Onions
Spinach
Squash
Sweet Potatoes
Yams
Tomatoes

Fruits

Apples
Cranberries
Blueberries
Grapefruit
Oranges
Pears
Plums
Rasberries
Watermelon
Strawberries

Grains

Barley
Brown Rice
Buckwheat
Corn
Millet
Oats
Quinoa
Rye
Spelt
Whole Wheat

Spices

Basil
Cilantro
Ginger
Oregano
Parsley
Peppermint
Rosemary
Sage
Thyme
Tumeric

Beans

Black Beans
Garbanzo Beans
Kidney Beans
Lima Beans
Miso
Pinto Beans
Navy Beans
Soy Beans
Tofu
Tempeh

Seafood

Cod
Halibut
Mackerel
Oysters
Salmons
Sardines
Scallops
Shrimp
Talapia
Tuna

Nuts

Almonds
Cashews
Flaxseed
Macadamia Nuts
Peanuts
Pistachios
Pumpkin Seeds
Sunflower Seeds
Sesame Seeds
Walnuts

Drinks

Cranberry Juice
Fat Free Milk
Fruit Smoothie
Green Tea
Mint Tea
Orange Juice
Soy Milk
Tomato Juice
Vegetable Juice
Water

MEET THE NEW **POWER FOODS**

Stock up on these ingredients. Research proves they can make you stronger, rev your metabolism, burn serious fat—even ease soreness so you can do it all over again tomorrow.

GAIN ENERGY

OATMEAL: Provides staying power so you won't crash between the 10th and 11th laps.

RAISINS: Grab a handful during long workouts for a natural energy boost.

BANANAS: Just as effective as sports drinks at keeping your electrolytes balanced.

SOOTHE PAIN

GINGER: Fights nausea and can reduce muscle pain by about 20 percent.

TART CHERRIES: They neutralize free radicals so you can recover faster.

TURMERIC: The spice that makes curry yellow acts like ibuprofen against joint pain.

BUILD MUSCLE

EGGS: This rich source of the amino acid leucine jump-starts muscle repair.

WHEY PROTEIN: Prime building material for tight abs and toned glutes.

SALMON OR TUNA: Their protein urges your muscles to begin the strenghening process.

PIKE METABOLISM

PISTACHIOS: Curb post-workout hunger without packing

BEETS: These bad boys help you push harder with less effort

EDAMAME: Soybeans are high in fat-torching protein

"healthy eating is a
journey that starts at
the grocery store ."

shopping list

How To Create A Healthy Grocery List

Grocery shopping can be a difficult task, even if you're the most organized person. And let's not talk about all the tempting unhealthy foods everywhere you turn threatening to throw you off your healthy eating goals. A grocery list is a helpful tool for navigating the store easily and helping you to stick to your healthy eating plan.

There are shopping list for the six weeks meal plan on the following pages. However, you will need to continue creating shopping list in the future. So, I have some tips that will help you prepare a healthy grocery shopping list so you can fill your cart with smart choices.

Plan Ahead
Having everything you need to prepare tasty meals all week long is an excellent way to maintain your healthy eating goals.

Keep a Running Grocery List
Rather than make a list every time you get ready to grocery shop, I keep a running list of the items I frequently buy. In the past I have also used apps made for grocery shopping and meal planning. Keeping a list of the items you use, as well as the new and healthy foods you want to try, will make putting your weekly shopping list together that much easier.

Organize Your List
Separating your grocery shopping list by category is a good way to save time and keep your shopping trips stress-free. I usually organize my list by food category and how my regular grocery stores are laid out.

Shopping List

Meats

3 lbs. Chicken Breast
20 Med. Shrimp
Pork Tender Lion
Fat Free Sliced Turkey Breast
Bag of Salmon Fillets
1 can of tuna
18 eggs

Seasonings/spices

Olive Oil
1 jar Minced Garlic
Ground Cumin
Onion Powder
Chili Powder
Cilantro
Lime
Corn Starch
Ginger
Cinnamon

Other Items:

100 calorie popcorn
100 Calorie nuts
100 Calorie Cookie's
Fiber one 70 Calorie brownies, cake, bars
Ole Xtreme Wraps
Mini wheat Pitas
Kashi 7 frozen waffles
Brown rice
Fat Free Cheddar Cheese
Oyster Sauce
Low Sodium Soy Sauce
Sesame Oil
Sriracha Sauce
Corn Starch
Baking Powder
Vanilla Extract
Instant Oatmeal packs
Non Fat Greek Yogurt
Sara Lee 45 calorie bread
Fat free salad dressing
quick-cook oats

Vegatables

Broccoli
Carrots
Spinach
kale
1 Canned Corn
1 can Black Beans
1 can Diced Tomatoes
Scallions
Bag of Garden Salad
Frozen Mixed Veggies
2 Small Sweet Pot.
Bananas
Apples
Grapes
Frozen Sliced Strawberries

Week Three and Four

Meats

4 lbs. Chicken Breast
1 pack of Canadian bacon
1 lbs. 98%Fat Free Ground
Turkey Breast
1 Salmon patty
24 eggs

seasonings/spices

1 taco season pack

Other items:

100 calorie popcorn
100 Calorie nuts
100 Calorie Cookie's
Fiber one 70 Calorie brownies, cake, bars
Ole Xtreme Wraps
Mini wheat Pitas
Kashi 7 frozen waffles
Brown Rice
Fat free cheddar cheese
Non Fat Greek Yogurt
Wheat pasta
Fat free gravy
Sweet potato chips
Hummus
Sara Lee 45 calorie bread

vegatables

1 can cannellini or pinto beans
1 Canned Corn
1 can Black Beans
Spinach
Carrots
1 can Green Beans
Diced Tomatoes w/chilies
Scallions
onion
1 Red bell pepper
1 can Kidney beans
Bag of Garden Salad
Avocado
Mango
Collard Greens
Bananas
Apples
Grapes
1 bag Cauliflower rice
1 8oz can tomato sauce
2 can dice tomatoes

Week Five and Six

Meats

2 lbs. Chicken Breast
1 pack of Canadian bacon
1 lbs. 98%Fat Free
GroundTurkey Breast
1 Salmon patty
1 Salmon fillet
1 can Shredded chicken breast
1 lbs. FF Sliced turkey breast
1 lb. Large shrimp
1lb. Pork tenderloin
1 Tilapia fillet
18 eggs

seasonings/spices

1 taco season pack
Cajun seasoning
Oregano
1 can chicken broth

Other items:

100 calorie popcorn
100 Calorie nuts
100 Calorie Cookie's
Fiber one 70 Calorie brownies, cake, bars
Ole Xtreme Wraps
Mini wheat Pitas
Kashi 7 frozen waffles
Brown Rice
Fat free cheddar cheese
Reduce fat shredded mozzarella cheese
Non Fat Greek Yogurt
Fat free gravy
Hummus
Sara Lee 45 calorie bread

vegatables

1 Canned Corn
1 Black Beans
Spinach
Carrots
Cilintro
Scallions
onion
Bag of Garden Salad
Avocado
Bananas
Apples
Grapes
3 bag Cauliflower rice
2 large tomatoes
1 can diced tomatoes
1 sweet potato
4 oz. can sliced mushrooms
Frozen Sliced Strawberries

PART 3

MEAL PREPARATION

Think about all the time you would save everyday if you didn't have to worry about finding recipes, buying groceries, and cooking every day. Instead of going through this exhausting daily routine, it's much easier when you choose to plan and prepare your meals in advance. This could mean making all three in batches or precooking all your food and portioning it out for the week in grab-and-go containers. The beauty of meal prepping is that it can be done on whatever cooking level you're at and made to fit your healthy eating goals.

The benefits of meal prepping.

Remove temptation.
Ever been hunger and have nothing around to eat? Yeah, and what was worse is that the only thing nearby was fast food or something unhealthy. Well, meal prepping helps you to have options that fit your healthy eating goals. This also makes it easier to stick to your goals.

Control over what you are eating.
When you are cooking your own meals or planning what to eat in advance, you get to be in total control. You gain complete calorie control, and you limit usage of unwanted ingredients like added sugar, salt, and fats. You are also ensuring you get the best-quality options and more fresh ingredients because you are selecting them yourself.

Save time.

When done properly, meal prepping can save a lot of time. I would cook all meals for the week each Sunday afternoon, and I when I would get home from work after a long day, I would be so thankful that I didn't have to go to the store or cook. This left me with more time to work out, relax or watch my favorite TV shows.

Save money.

Pricing out your food in advance is another piece of the meal-prep equation, which means your portion control now has cost control. You are saving money because you aren't ordering out every day for lunch or dinner and can choose your meal-prep recipes based on sales at the grocery store if you wish.

Manage hunger.

One of the benefits of meal prepping is that it helps you manage hunger. Meal prepping allows you to eat as soon as you feel hungry rather than having to wait and decide on what to eat. Managing hunger means you would be less likely to overeat when you finally sit down for a meal. When you feel as if you are starving you have a tendency to overeat.

Cooking Healthy

When starting a healthy eating journey, the best place to start is to cook more at home. When you cook at home you control the ingredients. Besides, restaurant meals are almost always higher in calories and sodium than something you would make yourself; this is how they make the food so tasteful. When you cook at home you get to make what you like, and how you like it! You can get similar results using healthier alternatives. If you're not sure how to start cooking healthier here are some of the things I did to make cooking healthy meals at home more enjoyable.

Learn new cooking methods and techniques.

I Brushed up on my skills with videos from YouTube and how-to articles.

The key to cooking healthy and tasty food is to find ways to maintain flavor while keeping the nutrients in the food.

I use my Air fryer for these healthier cooking methods:

- Baking: This method doesn't require added fat or moisture, which helps retain nutrients.
- Roasting: Another dry heat option that emphasizes low, slow cooking
- Air frying: It cuts calories by 70% to 80% and you use a lot less fat. Its healthier than oil frying while giving similar tasteful results.

You can make many of your favorite recipes healthier by using lower-fat or no-fat ingredients. These healthy substitutions can help you cut down on saturated or trans fats, without much difference in taste.

- Instead of whole milk (1 cup), use 1 cup fat-free or low-fat milk, plus one tablespoon of liquid vegetable oil.
- Instead of heavy cream (1 cup), use 1 cup evaporated skim milk or 1/2 cup low-fat yogurt and 1/2 cup plain low-fat unsalted cottage cheese.
- Instead of sour cream, use low-fat unsalted cottage cheese plus low-fat or fat-free yogurt; or just use fat-free sour cream.
- Instead of cream cheese, use 4 tablespoons soft margarine (low in saturated fat and 0 grams trans-fat) blended with 1 cup dry, unsalted low-fat cottage cheese; add a small amount of fat-free milk if needed.
- Instead of butter (1 tablespoon), use 1 tablespoon soft margarine (low in saturated fat and 0 grams trans fat) or 3/4 tablespoon liquid vegetable oil.
- Instead of unsweetened baking chocolate (1 ounce), use 3 tablespoons unsweetened cocoa powder or carob powder plus 1 tablespoon vegetable oil or soft margarine; since carob is sweeter than cocoa, reduce the sugar in the recipe by 25%.

Finding the time and energy to prepare home-cooked meals can seem like a grueling task. And somedays eating out might feel like the quickest, easiest option. But convenience and processed food can take a toll on the castle mentally and physically. There are plenty of quick, simple, and healthy meals you can cook at home in less time than it takes to travel to a restaurant or wait for a delivery. Whatever your abilities are as a cook, you can learn to prepare quick and healthy meals that can have real benefits for your mental and physical health.

What About Portion Control

 Portion control is the only way to make sure you're eating enough nutritious food and aren't overeating, while helping you reach your health eating goals.

But first you must understand portions, how much to eat to feel satisfied, and stay energized until your next meal. This is different from knowing what a "serving" or "serving size", which is the recommended amount of a specific food you should eat.

Become familiar with the correct portion size for you and your healthy eating goals, you won't need to measure your food servings at each meal. It takes practice, but eating the right amount will eventually become part of your daily meal prep habits.

Using smaller dinner plates at home can help you control your portions and feel satisfied after eating a full plate of food.

When you don't have access to measuring utensils, you can estimate a portion size based on your hand size. Your hand is proportional to your body, making this a useful guide.

- Your palm is the size of a portion of good quality protein.
- Your fist is approximately the size of a portion of vegetables.
- Your cupped hand indicates a portion of carbohydrates.
- A portion of healthy fats should be the size of your thumb.

Starting each meal with a glass of water can help address thirst disguised as hunger.

Use a smaller plate and only fill it once, keeping your food proportions in mind to ensure you are following your healthy eating goals.

YOUR HAND IS YOUR PORTIONING TOOL

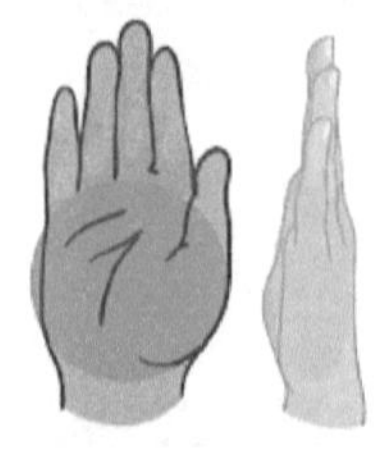

A serving of protein = 1 palm

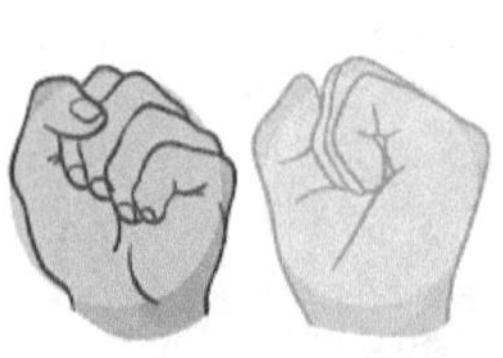

A serving of vegetables = 1 fist

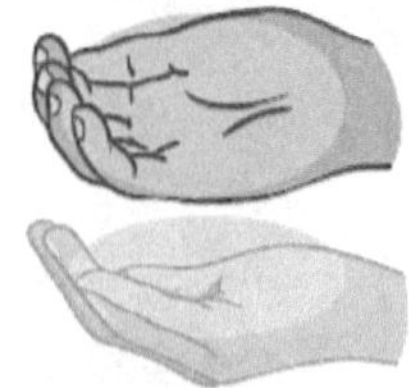

A serving of carbs = 1 cupped hand

A serving of fats = 1 thumb

Prepping for Meal Prep

Studies have shown that people who meal prep for the week eat healthier and lower body weight than those who don't. Plus, those who plan their meals ahead of time tend to cook more meals at home, a practice that has been linked to healthier eating and healthier weight. As I stated earlier making a point to plan your meals for the week can help you avoid making unhealthy eating choices and help you create a grocery shopping list more cost efficient. Below is my method for getting started.

5 Steps to Getting Started

1. Choose a specific day of the week to plan the menu, write out your grocery list, food shop, do the meal prep, and most of your cooking. Some of these tasks can be done on the same day, but breaking up these tasks may help keep meal planning manageable.

2. On your meal prep day, focus first on foods that take the longest to cook, usually it's the proteins.

3. Multi-task! While foods are baking or cooking, chop vegetables and fresh fruit, or wash and dry salad greens for later in the week.

4. When you cook a recipe, make extra portions for another day or two of meals, or to freeze for a different week. Be sure to date and label what goes in the freezer so you know what you have on hand.

5. For lunches, get a head-start and use individual meal containers. Divide cooked food into the containers on prep day.

Storage

Whether you prep your food on Sunday or you're storing leftovers to take to work the next day, choosing the right container is important. How you store your food can make a huge difference between a fresh, tasty meal and a spoiled, distasteful one. I use containers that are freezer, microwave, and oven-safe to make sure I'm able to heat my food under different circumstances. So, let's talk about what to store the meals in and how.

I use Rubbermaid Brilliance Food Storage containers because they are versatile, durable, affordable, lightweight, and easy to store. Plus, they're designed to prevent staining and are safe for the freezer, microwave, and dishwasher. These containers in a set of 10 can be found on Amazon for a little over $33. Below is an actual picture.

After storing your meals label all prepped items with a date so that you can keep track when to use them. Make sure you are eating the oldest meals first. Store greens, herbs, and chopped fruits at eye-level so you remember to use them.

Below are the recommended times to store your cooked foods to offer the best flavors, maximum nutrients, and food safety.

Refrigeration at 40°F or lower
- Cooked ground poultry or ground beef for 1-2 days
- Cooked whole meats, fish and poultry; soups and stews for 3-4 days
- Cooked beans; hummus for 5 days
- Hard boiled eggs/chopped vegetables stored in air-tight container for 1 week
- Soft cheese, opened for 2 weeks
- Hard cheese, opened for 5-6 weeks

Freezing at 0°F or lower
- Soups and stews; cooked beans for 2-3 months
- Cooked or ground meat and poultry for 3-6 months
- Berries and chopped fruit stored in a freezer bag for 6-8 months
- Vegetables, if blanched first for about 3-5 minutes (depending on the vegetable) for 8-12 month

Meal prepping is a form of choice architecture. Choice architecture is setting up situations to make good choices easier. For example, I keep chips in a high cabinet out of my eyesight or I don't buy them at all. Choice architecture is a strategy that could help keep you on track.

More examples:
- Keeping foods out of the house that you tend to overeat.
- Making meals in advance so, they've available when you get hangry.
- Planning a dinner out in advance so that you can look. at the menu and choose a meal prior to going.

"meal prep once...
eat healthy all week."

meal prep

How To Make Meal Prepping Fun

You may dread just the thought of meal prepping. This process is definitely going to feel like a chore. I know from experience! And at one point I had to figure out ways to keep it fun in order to continue and stay motivated.

Here are four things I did to keep my pep while I prepped.

1.   My favorite is to poor a glass of wine (or 2). I usually poor a glass of wine to sip on while cooking if it is to meal prep or prepare a single meal. It relaxes me and helps to get me in the mood for the task.

2.   Playing music is a must. It keeps me moving and hypes me up.

3.   I clean as I go to prevent getting frustrated. The clean-up from meal prepping is a whole other task in itself.

4.   Last but not least. If you know me, you know that mindset plays apart in everything that I do. You can try all you want to make meal prepping fun but if you view it as a daunting chore, it will be just that. Shift your mindset and view it as self-care, a gift of good food, and a gift of being and feeling prepared for your week.

Week One Meal Plan

Monday

Morning snack: Apple
Afternoon snack: 100 calorie pack cookies

Oatmeal
BREAKFAST

Non Fat Greek Yogurt w/Strawberries&Ban
LUNCH

Shrimp Taco Bowl
DINNER

Tuesday

Morning snack: Banana
Afternoon snack: 100 calorie pack popcorn

2 boiled Eggs w/ 2 Slices of Sara Lee bread toatsed
BREAKFAST

Garden salad and fresh fruits
LUNCH

Chicken and Broccoli Stir Fry
DINNER

Wednesday

Morning snack: Fruit Bowl

Afternoon snack: Fiber one 70 calorie brownie

Banana Pancakes
BREAKFAST

Tuna Over Garden Salad
LUNCH

Roasted Salmon over Brown Rice w/Broccoli
DINNER

Thursday

Morning snack: Apple

Afternoon snack: 100 Calorie Pack Cookie

Veggie Egg White Omelette and toast
BREAKFAST

Baked Sweet Potatoe
LUNCH

Chicken and Broccoli Stir Fry
DINNER

Friday

Morning snack: Banana

Afternoon snack: 100 calorie pack popcorn

oatmeal
BREAKFAST

Grill Chicken on Ole Xtreme Wrap
LUNCH

Shrimp Taco Bowl
DINNER

Week Two Meal Plan

Monday

Morning snack: **Banana**

Afternoon snack: Fiber One 90 Calorie Bar

Bannana Pancakes
BREAKFAST

Non fat Greek Yogurt w/Strawberries&Ban
LUNCH

Chicken and Broccoli Stir Fry
DINNER

Tuesday

Morning snack: Fruit Bowl

Afternoon snack: 100 Calorie Pack Popcorn

Kashi 7 Frozen Waffles
BREAKFAST

Sliced Turkey Breast In A Mini Whole Wheat Pita
LUNCH

Pork Tender Loin Small sweet Pot. w/ Kale
DINNER

Wednesday

Morning snack: Apple

Afternoon snack: 100 Calorie Pack Nuts

Oatmeal
BREAKFAST

Grilled Chicken Ole wrap
LUNCH

ShrimpTaco Bowl
DINNER

Thursday

Morning snack: 1 cup of Grapes

Afternoon snack: Fiber One 70 Calorie Cin.Cake

Egg White Burrito
BREAKFAST

Garden salad and fresh fruits
LUNCH

Chicken and Broccoli Stir Fry
DINNER

Friday

Morning snack: Banana

Afternoon snack: 100 Calorie Pack Popcorn

Spinach Egg White Omeltte
BREAKFAST

ShrimpTaco Bowl
LUNCH

Salmon w/ Mixed Veggies
DINNER

Week Three Meal Plan

Monday

Morning snack: Fruit Bowl

Afternoon snack: Carrots and Hummus

Non fat Greek Yogurt w/Strawberries&Ban
BREAKFAST

Taco Soup
LUNCH

Grilled chicken diced tomatoes over wheat garlic pasta
DINNER

Tuesday

Morning snack: Banana

Afternoon snack: 100 calorie almond pack

2 slices of Canadian bacon w/2 boiled eggs
BREAKFAST

Salmon over brown rice W/ FF gravy
LUNCH

Tuna Caesar salad and fresh fruits
DINNER

Wednesday

Morning snack: Apple

Afternoon snack: 70c Fiber one bar

Kashi 7 Frozen Waffles
BREAKFAST

Sriracha cauliflower fried rice
LUNCH

Diced tomatoes & ground turkey on wheat pasta
DINNER

Thursday

Morning snack: Grapes

Afternoon snack: Non fat Greek yogurt w/honey

Tomato and spinach omelet with toast
BREAKFAST

Taco Soup
LUNCH

Turkey burger with sweet potato chips
DINNER

Friday

Morning snack: Banana

Afternoon snack: 100c popcorn

Oatmeal
BREAKFAST

Non fat Greek Yogurt w/Strawberries&Ban
LUNCH

Sriracha cauliflower fried rice
DINNER

Week Four Meal Plan

Monday

Morning snack: 1/2 grapefriut

Afternoon snack:100 calorie almond pack

Banana pancakes
BREAKFAST

Collard wrap grill chicken avocado w/ mangos
LUNCH

Sriracha cauliflower fried rice
DINNER

Tuesday

Morning snack: Apple

Afternoon snack: Carrots and Hummus

Breakfast Burrito
BREAKFAST

Taco Soup
LUNCH

Grill chicken over garlic wheat pasta
DINNER

Wednesday

Morning snack:1/2 grapefriut

Afternoon snack: Non fat Greek yogurt w/honey

2 slices of Canadian bacon w/2 boiled eggs
BREAKFAST

Turkey burger with garden Salad
LUNCH

Salmon over brown rice W/ FF gravy
DINNER

Thursday

Morning snack:Banana

Afternoon snack:70c Fiber one bar

Breakfast Burrito
BREAKFAST

Collard wrap grill chicken avocado w/ mangos
LUNCH

Salmon burger with sweet potato chips
DINNER

Friday

Morning snack: Grapes

Afternoon snack:100c popcorn

Kashi 7 Frozen Waffles
BREAKFAST

Taco Soup
LUNCH

Sriracha cauliflower fried rice
DINNER

Week Five Meal Plan

Monday

Morning snack: Fruit Bowl

Afternoon snack: Carrots and hummus

Oatmeal
BREAKFAST

Blackened tilapia over garden salad
LUNCH

Cheesy Chicken cauliflower skillet
DINNER

Tuesday

Morning snack: Banana

Afternoon snack:100c popcorn

Breakfast Burrito
BREAKFAST

Grill Chicken on Ole Xtreme Wrap
LUNCH

Turkey Taco Bowl with Cauliflower Rice
DINNER

Wednesday

Morning snack:70c Fiber one bar

Afternoon snack: 1 cup Pineapples

Veggie Omelet
BREAKFAST

Cauliflower shrimp and grits
LUNCH

Pork Tender Lion with FF gravy over brown rice
DINNER

Thursday

Afternoon snack:100 Calorie Pack Cookie

Morning snack: Apple w/1TBS of peanute butter

Canadian bacon and toast
BREAKFAST

Sliced Turkey Breast In A Mini Whole Wheat Pita
LUNCH

Turkey Taco Bowl with Cauliflower Rice
DINNER

Friday

Morning snack:1 cup Pineapples

Afternoon snack: 70c Fiber one bar

Non fat Greek Yogurt w/Strawberries & Banana
BREAKFAST

Cauliflower shrimp and grits
LUNCH

Cheesy Chicken cauliflower skillet
DINNER

Week Six Meal Plan

Monday

Morning snack:Apple w/1TBS of peanute butter

Afternoon snack:70c Fiber one cake

Scrambled eggs spinach and 3 oz chicken breast
BREAKFAST

Garden salad and fresh fruits
LUNCH

Cheesy Chicken cauliflower skillet
DINNER

Tuesday

Morning snack: Fruit Bowl

Afternoon snack:100 Calorie Pack Cookie

Oatmeal
BREAKFAST

Salmon burger on Sara Lee bread
LUNCH

Turkey Taco Bowl with Cauliflower Rice
DINNER

Wednesday

Morning snack: Banana

Afternoon snack:100c popcorn

fat Greek Yogurt w/Strawberries&Ban
BREAKFAST

Grill Chicken on Ole Xtreme Wrap
LUNCH

Diced tomatoes over salmon and brown rice
DINNER

Thursday

Morning snack:1/2 Grapefruit

Afternoon snack: Carrots and hummus

FF cheddar cheese omelet and toast
BREAKFAST

Baked sweet potato
LUNCH

Turkey Taco Bowl with Cauliflower Rice
DINNER

Friday

Morning snack:1/2 Grapefruit

Afternoon snack:Non fat Greek yogurt w/honey

Scrambled eggs spinach and 3 oz chicken breast
BREAKFAST

Turkey Breast In A Mini Whole Wheat Pita
LUNCH

Cheesy Chicken cauliflower skillet
DINNER

PART **4**

HEALTHY FOOD ON THE GO

"eat crappy, feel crappy. eat healthy, feel healthy."

How To Eat Healthy On The Go

We are all busy, and let's face it there will be times you may not feel like meal prepping or cooking a single meal for the day and you may only have time to eat on the go. Choosing to eat on the go doesn't have to mean your sacrificing your healthy eating goals. As I have stated earlier when setting your healthy eating goals or trying to start more healthy eating habits, the first things you have to do is be honest with yourself about, your time, foods you truly enjoy and the ones you dislike, and the barriers that could hinder your progress.

When you know it's going to be a busy day, pack a good snack. It can keep you from overeating later in the day. Be careful because some snacks may seem healthy, but still may be high in carbs, added sugars, fat, and sodium have little nutritional value. So, remember to use the tools that you learned in part one on reading the nutrient labels. Keep snacks such as unsalted nuts (walnuts, almonds, peanuts, cashews, etc.) on hand. These snacks are great sources of the healthy fats and protein that I spoke about earlier. My favorite is preparing vegetable snacks with hummus or salsa.

Going out to dinner is a fun and enjoyable part of life that I would never recommend restricting yourself from, but there's no denying that eating out on a regular basis could mean consuming to many calories or foods high in fat, sugar, or sodium and that would not be beneficial to your healthy eating goals. The key is to have mindful tools to implement before eating out.

Try to schedule the days you're going to eat out, make it something special you can look forward to. Look at the menu online in advance, you want to check out your healthy options before you get there to avoid making a choice that isn't a part of you're healthy eating goals.

Drink plenty of water before you eat, it's easy to overeat if you confuse your body's thirst signals for hunger. Water also helps with digestion.

Choose healthier dishes that are baked, steamed, roasted, pan-fried, boiled, or grilled rather than deep fried.

 Try to view the menu in the perspective of what will nourish your body and make you feel good, instead of viewing foods as good or bad. Remember mindset is important!!!

You can always order just an appetizer instead of full meal, order small or medium instead of large. There have been times that I have ordered the child's plate or meal to prevent overeating and to control my calorie intake while dining out.

Most importantly if your options are limited or you overeat, don't beat yourself up. Focus on your healthy eating goals as a whole. If you experience food guilt, document in your food and mood journal. Then shift your mindset to feelings of gratitude for your meal, who you ate with, and the joy and ability to dine out. It's a privilege not everyone has!

You can make healthy choices when you eat out by choosing lower-fat foods instead.

At a Restaurant

- Instead of cream-based soups, try broth-based soups with lots of vegetables.
- Instead of a burger and fries, try soup and salad.
- Instead of buffalo chicken wings, try peel-and-eat shrimp.
- Instead of bread, muffins, or croissants, try pita bread, or whole-grain rolls.
- Instead of a fried chicken sandwich, try a grilled chicken sandwich.
- Instead of chicken fried steak, try a veggie burger.
- Instead of French fries, try baked potato, brown rice, or steamed vegetables.
- Instead of potatoes and gravy, try potatoes without gravy or a baked potato.
- Instead of creamy coleslaw, try sautéed vegetables, steamed vegetables or a tossed salad.
- Instead of a hot fudge sundae or ice cream, try nonfat yogurt, sherbet or fruit ice.

For Fast-Food

- Instead of a Danish, try a small bagel.
- Instead of a jumbo cheeseburger, try a grilled chicken sandwich, or a regular hamburger on a bun with lettuce, tomato and onion.
- Instead of fried chicken, try a grilled chicken and a side salad.
- Instead of fried chicken pieces, try a grilled chicken sandwich.
- Instead of French fries, try a baked potato with vegetables and/or low-fat or fat-free sour cream or margarine on the side.

diet vs. Healthy Eating Lifestyle
PART 5

Diet or Healthy Eating?

There is a difference between a healthy eating lifestyle and being on a diet. A diet is temporarily changing your eating habits for weight loss, and then returning to your previous eating habits. A healthy eating lifestyle is adopting overall healthy eating habits that promote long-term health. Diets tend to focus on food intake, while healthy lifestyle habits incorporate what you eat along with physical activity. Where weight loss is concerned, a diet provides a temporary solution.

Dieting does not provide the proper tools for long term weight loss. Diets can help you lose weight in the short term. But it's unlikely that you'll maintain the weight loss once you go back to your regular eating habits. Most people regain all the weight they release after dieting, plus more, according to the research. Researchers found lifestyle changes contributed to the ability to keep the weight off. These behavior patterns included eating breakfast regularly, exercising an average of 30 min each day, maintaining consistent healthy eating patterns during the week and on weekends, keeping tabs on and eating a relatively low-fat, low-calorie foods.

Healthy eating is freeing and means choosing a food because, in that moment, it feels like a nutritious choice. When I choice a food my focus is pleasure, appetite, and the nutrients of the food. Most importantly, I'm making my own food choices, formulated from a perspective of self-care and not self-control. Overall health and well-being are my objective, not focusing on changing my body or releasing weight.

Breaking The Diet Mindset

When you're in a diet mindset, you're more focused on rules around eating rather than choosing foods that are healthy. Some characteristics of a dieting mindset are:

- Banning foods
- Cutting out foods you enjoy eating that provide good nutritional value (example cutting out fruit)
- Thinking of food as either good or bad
- All or nothing thinking.
- Your main priority is reaching a number on the scales or certain body fat percentage, rather than being healthy.
- Using pills/potions/detox teas for fat loss.

A diet mindset usually leads to feelings of guilt and anxiety. You lose touch with your intuitions with food and rely more on "fixing you" and what you should and shouldn't eat. This is how the cycle of dieting, overeating, guilt and feeling out of control starts. The good news is you can get out of this cycle! It takes a big shift in mindset to break this cycle, but it is possible.

Here's how to start shifting your mindset:

1.   It's important to know that food isn't good or bad. Food doesn't have a moral value! View them as everyday foods and pleasure foods. Eating chocolate, or chips, or whatever it is you enjoy isn't bad. It isn't going to ruin your health. No food is 'fattening' or bad for your health unless you eat too much of it. Don't ban foods. It's the fastest way to bring on food cravings. Resistance causes the reverse effect. The power of the food is reduced once you allow yourself to eat it.

You can eat the foods you enjoy and still maintain a healthy weight and healthy eating habits. It's about moderation, and although this isn't the fad, you will see how much easier it is to reach your goals.

2.   Find your own healthy balance. The best way to eat is to follow a pattern that works for you. Find a healthy eating pattern that works for you. Sometimes, getting help is the best answer. Seeing a registered nutritionist or a dietitian, you don't have to do it alone.

3.   Make an effort to start eating your meals more mindfully. Turn off the TV or computer. Sit down and enjoy the experience of eating. Eat your food slowly. When you eat your favorite foods mindfully, rather than feeling guilty about it, you may find that you are satisfied with less and enjoy it more.

4.   When weight is the sole focus of lifestyle change, it's easy to go back to old eating habits if you don't see results. Focusing on health and well-being is not dictated by a number, rather than by behaviors and feelings of wellness. These goals are more positive, and of more beneficial.

Being Healthy Is A Lifestyle

It's common to think that eating healthy and exercising are the only factors to being healthy. In reality, creating a healthy lifestyle and maintaining it isn't about just those two factors. It's also about having a positive mindset, strong mental health, and a healthy body image (which I will touch on next). You also need to get enough sleep, surround yourself with positive people, and avoid the things that trigger unproductive behaviors.

A healthy lifestyle is what allows you to move through your journey successfully and with ease. Making healthy choices isn't always going to be easy. I'm here to tell you it's going to be moments when it's going to be hard to find the time and energy to exercise regularly, prepare healthy meals, and just simply make healthy choice for your mental and physical. However, your efforts will pay off in many ways, take one day at time, and remember to have compassion for yourself and you will be just fine on your journey to transformation.

A healthy lifestyle simply means doing things that make you happy and feel good. For me that's working out three times a week, going out to dinner once a week with my best friend, listening to high frequency music every day, spending time with my partner, and working with my clients during the week. For someone else, that might be training for and running two marathons a year, becoming a vegan, and never having a sip of alcohol. Healthy lifestyles will vary from person to person and may even vary at difference stage in your life. Nevertheless one life style isn't better than the other. Both are perfect for that person. You get to decide what your healthy lifestyle looks like.

Here are some important reminders and ways to help you remember that eating healthy does not mean restricting yourself.

There are moments in life like birthdays, graduations, Sunday night family dinner traditions, or a dinner with friends when we celebrated with foods, and sharing food with loved ones is a vital part of the bonding experience. Certain food choices are even part of the cultural background and traditions. It is important to note that when the goal of eating healthy starts to negatively impact or limit these special moments in life, it might be time to re-evaluate your methods and mindset.

Again, what you tell yourself is important. Continue to keep your thoughts positive. Use the affirmations located in part six as needed.

I believe in the 80/20 rule. The 80-20 rule states that 20% of what you do will result in 80% of the outcomes. In this case, focus on your healthy eating goals as part of a healthy lifestyle 80 to 90 percent of the time, and give yourself permission to enjoy and indulge 10 to 20 percent of the time.

It is important that we cultivate healthy eating habits with room for moderation and indulgences. This approach can not only remove the stress that comes along with dieting but also helps you to enjoy foods without putting restriction on your lifestyle.

Healthy Body Image

Part 6

"sexy is a mindset
not a waist size."

Loving The Skin Your In

The American Psychological Association defines body image as how you see your body's physical characteristics and your attitude toward these characteristics. These days the definition of having a "healthy" body image can be more difficult in a culture where celebrities, social media influencers, and experts all have opinions that are more ego driven. But it's just this simple, a healthy body image is a body image where you feel happy and confident and accepting of yourself. This doesn't mean that you'll never have a moment when you will express a concern about your body. This doesn't even necessarily mean that you'll want to celebrate or love every inch of your body. But it does mean that your complaints or concerns about your body, whatever they are, aren't leaving you with body issues that preventing you from living a peaceful quality of life.

At the end of the day, I haven't met anyone that doesn't have something they would like to change about their bodies. But you'll be happier if you focus on the things you like about your body. If you start to criticize your body, tell yourself to stop. Instead, think about what you like about yourself, both inside and out. Use the "Diva's Don't Deflect, They Journal" confidence journal to bring awareness to your thoughts.

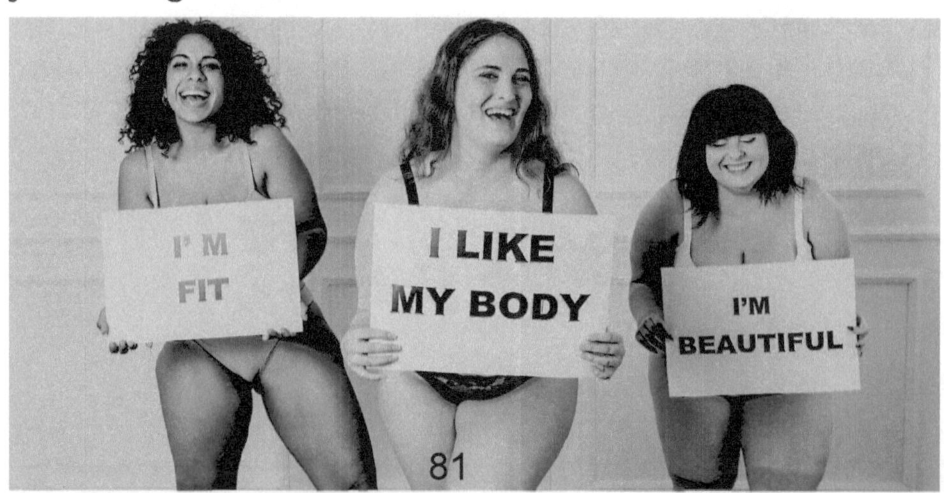

81

And hey, your body isn't just a place to hang your clothes! It can do some truly amazing things. So, focus on how strong and healthy your body is or can be. It's the day and age of social media. And it's a gift and a curse! Don't allow the models and actresses on social media to affect how you think you should look. They get lots of help from makeup artists, personal trainers, and they do a lot of photo shopping to their pictures. And advertisers often focus on body image to get people to buy their crap. Don't let them F with your mindset!

It's never just one tool you need to learn or implement that can help you reach your goals. There will always be a collective of information and things you need to do to help you maintain this journey of healthy living. My next set of tips aren't going to magically turn your negative body thoughts into positive body image, but it will introduce you to healthier ways of looking at yourself and your body. The more you practice these new thought patterns, the better you will feel about who you are and the body you naturally have.

Shift your thoughts to how your body performs, not what it looks like.
Try changing your focus from weight and shape to all the other aspects of your life that you enjoy, whether that's being a good friend, playing a sport you love, or volunteering for a good cause. Make a conscious effort to appreciate the way your body is right now.

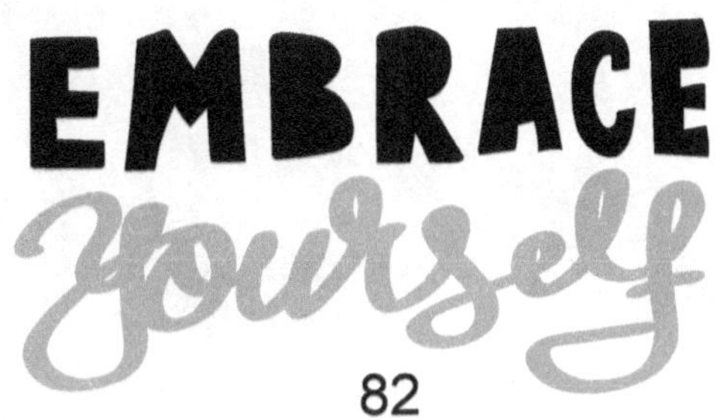

Be Realistic About Your Individual Size

The majority of us, even at a healthy and fit weight, will not have a body that looks like a supermodel or professional athlete. And to think that is unrealistic. The myth that everybody can be like that if we try hard enough, just buy the right product, or work out hard enough is just that a myth. And if we cannot physically achieve that goal, not only do we start disliking ourselves, but we also start beating ourselves up. This book is about creating healthy goals because that's what you should do. But recognize that no matter how many healthy goals you accomplish you're not going to be able to transform your body into a 6-foot supermodel. I'm 5 foot 1 inches tall and curvy, it's just not going to happen!

Don't be fooled by what you see on tv and social media.
The images we see on tv and social media will have us feeling like there is only one standard of beauty. And the images don't even represent real life, thanks to make up and photo retouching. And on top of that, they don't represent the diversity of people and their bodies. That exist in this world. **THERE IS NOT JUST ONE DEFINITION OF BEAUTY!**

Embrace body neutrality if body positivity feels farfetched.
Having a neutral body image may be more realistic than positive body image for you. "The term body neutrality" is not having to love your body to respect it, nourish it, listen to its cues, or to have gratitude for what it can do.

Take a stand against body shaming.
Body shaming is hurtful. And while it may be difficult to confront someone who is body shaming you, someone else, or even themselves, if someone is making body shaming comments speak up and let them know it's not ok. Be the change your tribe needs. How you respond could affect your own body image. Research has shown that challenging fat talk, or body shaming can lessen the blow even when the negativity was aimed at someone else.

Seek help from a professional if body image Is taking over with your life.
Being dissatisfied with your body from time to time is normal. But when the dissatisfaction continues not addressing it can lead to bigger issues. A therapist or life coach can help you create strategies and tools to change your negative self-talk. Don't be afraid to reaching out to a professional to improve your body image. The sooner you start having the conversations the better. The longer you stay in your own head, the harder it may be to create a healthier mindset. It's important to connect with someone who can challenge your interpretation of reality. The more isolated you become, the more ingrained the beliefs become.

If you're struggling here are some signs that you should consider talking to a life coach or therapist to get some coping skills that will help you manage body image issues:

When your negative self-talk is extreme or outrageous.
It's one thing to say to yourself, "Ugh, my stomach drives me nuts." But it's another issue if you regularly use stronger language, like: "I hate myself because I'm fat." If your self-talk has moved beyond the realm of irritation or frustration, and it feels more like body hatred, it's time to seek help.

When you avoid leaving the house.
If you're avoiding or not enjoying social events because the way your body looks, that's a red flag. Your body image concerns are getting in the way of you living your life, it's time to seek help.

When you obsess about certain body parts.
Obsessing about a part of your body may be a red flag. This obsession could possibly be a mental health disorder. To maintain mental wellness, speak to a therapist to ensure that your obsession is not or has not developed into a mental health concern.

When the people around you raise concerns.
If people who love you are saying, "Excuse me, but that's too much, you're hurting yourself, or you're being too hard on yourself". It is time to get help.

When negative thoughts turn into harmful actions
Are you making extreme changes to your eating or fitness routine with the goal of getting your body to look a very specific way? This behavior can quickly move into the unhealthy or harmful zone. If you are constantly dieting, binge-eating, purging, or over-exercising. Please get help!!!!

And now that we've gotten that out the way, your body deserves a treat!!! It's time to take a nice bubble bath, do some stretching, or just curl up on a comfy couch with a comfy blanket. Do something soothing like get a massage.

Affirmations to Embrace Body Positivity

I LOVE AND ACCEPT MY BODY AS IT IS TODAY.

ALL BODIES ARE BEAUTIFUL, INCLUDING MINE.

THANK THE FOOD I EAT FOR NOURISHING MY BODY.

PROGRESS IS NOT MEASURED BY A NUMBER ON A SCALE.

I AM NOT DEFINED BY MY WEIGHT OR APPEARANCE.

I AM DEFINED BY WHO I AM ON THE INSIDE.

TODAY, I DECLARE THAT I LOVE MY_________ BECAUSE OF ITS________

I AM GRATEFUL FOR WHAT MY BODY IS CAPABLE OF DOING.

I FEEL PROUD OF HOW FAR I'VE COME.

Healthy Weight Maintenance

There are many factors that can affect your weight, including your genes, age, gender, lifestyle, habits, culture, sleep, and even where you live and work. Some of these factors can make it hard to maintain or achieve a healthy weight. Regardless, following a nutritious eating pattern and exercising regularly can help keep your body as healthy as possible for your age range.

Being active and choosing healthy foods can help you maintain or achieve a healthy weight, feel more energetic, and decrease your chances of having other health problems. It's important to choose foods filled with nutrients and aim for at least 30 minutes of physical activity a day.

If you notice through out the book I use the word release weight not loss weight. changing your words and what you put out into universe matters. If you say or use the word loss that insinuates that something is lost or can't be found and subconsciously you look for things that are lost. If we are looking to get rid of unwanted weight it is not lost!

Now lets talk about how stress and sleep can impact releasing or maintaining healthy weight. Stress has a significant impact on the body's ability to release unwanted as well weight. So, find ways to get into your zone of peace, calm, and presence. This might mean connecting with nature, interacting with friends, journaling, going for a walk, meditating, or energy healing. These activities put your body into a relaxed space that your body should be in while cooking and eating meals.

We have a circadian rhythm that is a 24-hour cycle a part of the body's internal clock that syncs with the rising and setting of the sun. This plays a significant role in weight release. Thyroid, estrogen, progesterone, testosterone, and insulin are all hormones that strongly impact metabolism and other processes related to weight management, and they are produced at night. So, when you go to sleep before 11 pm, you benefit from the body's sleep hormone, melatonin, which is the body's most potent self-made antioxidant. If you work from home, separating work and relaxation can be challenging, and sleep patterns can be thrown off. For a good night's rest, be sure to turn off electronics at least an hour before bed, avoid working from your bedroom, find activities to help you wind down.

At the end of the day, you don't need to spend a lot of money joining a gym or hiring a personal trainer to get fit. Think about the kinds of physical activities that you enjoy, for example, walking, running, bicycling, gardening, swimming, and dancing. Even everyday chores such as vacuuming can provide physical activity. While you're getting started with this new healthy lifestyle try to stay motivated to move your body regularly. Then increase the length of time you exercise or add another fun activity. And don't forget to get at least 7 hours of sleep. Using the healthy weight tracker on the following page will also help you work towards your healthy weight.

Small Changes That Can Help You L~~o~~se Weight Release

✗ If you usually...	✓ Instead you can...	If you make this change...	You could lose up to this many pounds a year
✗ Use the elevator or escalator	✓ Climb stairs for 2 minutes	Every day	2
✗ Use a tablespoon of mayonnaise on your sandwich	✓ Use mustard	3 times a week	4
✗ Eat a *large* order of fast food fries	✓ Substitute a *small* order of fast food fries	Once a week	5
✗ Watch a lot of TV	✓ Do a little housework	1/2 hour a day	5
✗ Drink an 8-oz. glass of *whole* milk	✓ Drink an 8-oz. glass of non-*fat* milk	Once a day	6
✗ Have 2 drinks sitting at the bar for an hour	✓ Order 1 drink and dance for an hour	Once a week	6
✗ Drive or take a taxi, bus or subway	✓ Walk briskly for 20 minutes	Every day	7
✗ Snack on a 2-oz. chocolate bar	✓ Have a piece of fruit	Twice a week	7
✗ Drink a 16-oz. latte with *whole* milk	✓ Drink a 16-oz. latte with non-*fat* milk	Every day	10
✗ Eat a 3-egg cheese omelet with bacon, toast and hash browns	✓ Have a bowl of cereal with non-*fat* milk for breakfast	Once a week	11
✗ Eat a pint of ice cream every week	✓ Substitute a half-pint of sorbet	Every week	12
✗ Drink a can of regular soda	✓ Have a glass of water	Once a day	15

HEALTHY WEIGHT TRACKER

MONTH: YEAR:

DATE	WEIGHT	GAIN+	LOSS+	NOTES

"eat to fill your stomach, not your heart."

FOOD & MOOD

MINI Journal

HEALTHY
FOOD
HEALTHY
LIFESTYLE

Understanding what triggers you to emotional eating can help you take control of the behavior. Sometimes we eat to satisfy physical hunger, but oftentimes, it's to satisfy an emotional need or fill a void as I stated in part 2 of the book. For the most part we are unaware of the triggers that cause us to eat when we're not really hungry.

Use this tracker to keep a record of what you eat and drink (including alcoholic and non-alcoholic drinks) for the next 21 days to help you identify the triggers that make you want to eat when you are not physically hungry. Continue tracking for another 21 one days making conscious decisions to make better eating choices.

How to use the journal

1.   Time: Write down what time you ate the meal or snack or consumed each drink.

2.   Who, what, why? Write down who you were with; what you were doing; and why you ate or drank the specific meal.

3.   Thought: Write down what your thoughts were.

4.   What Was Your Mood? How were you feeling when you ate or drank the item ? Refer to the emotion images and write down the name of the feeling under the emotion picture. If your mood is not listed, write in your own description.

5.   What Was Your Level of Hunger? (Applies to food only.) How hungry were you when you ate?   On a scale of 1-10.

6.   If you felt that there was a consequence for the poor food choice write it down.

7.   What did you really need at the time? Ex. A hug, something to do, a pick me up etc.

No, for real… How do you actually feel?

Identifying your emotions can be a difficult thing to because you can't identify what you don't know! It's easy to say you are feeling "good" or "happy" "mad" or "sad". However, how you are truly feeling and why is often much more complicated to identify with. So, on the next page is a chart to use as a tool to help you figure it out.

Start with these three simple steps to identify your true emotions:

1. Make a habit of checking in throughout the day. You might notice that you feel excited after making plans to go on a date, upset at something a coworker said, or you might be relaxed when listening to high frequency music. Notice whatever emotion you feel, then name that emotion in your mind. Notice that each emotion passes and makes room for the next experience.
2. Rate how strong the feeling is. After you notice and name an emotion, take it a step further: Rate how strongly you feel the emotion on a scale of 1–10, with 1 being the mildest feeling and 10 the most intense.
3. Share your feelings with the people closest to you. This is the best way to practice putting emotions into words, a skill that helps us feel closer to friends or our partners. Make it a daily practice to share feelings with loved ones.

Time To Check In

Right Now I feel...

AFRAID

SAD

WORRIED

HAPPY

ASHAMED

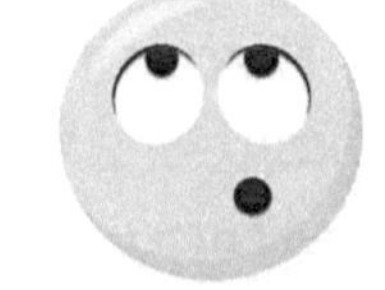

DISTRACTED

EMBARRASSED

NERVOUS

CONFIDENT

FRUSTRATED

GUILTY

LONELY

EXHAUSTED

SURPRISED

SHY

CONFUSED

PROUD

SHOCKED

ANGRY

OVERWHELMED

Food and Mood Journal

Date Time	Trigger? What caused you to eat?	What food/ drink?	Thoughts? What were you thinking?	Feelings? How did you feel?	Hunger? How hungry? What type of hunger?	Consequences? Short term? Long Term?	What did you really need?

Date Time	Trigger? What caused you to eat?	What food/ drink?	Thoughts? What were you thinking?	Feelings? How did you feel?	Hunger? How hungry? What type of hunger?	Consequences? Short term? Long Term?	What did you really need?

Food and Mood Journal

Date Time	Trigger? What caused you to eat?	What food/ drink?	Thoughts? What were you thinking?	Feelings? How did you feel?	Hunger? How hungry? What type of hunger?	Consequences? Short term? Long Term?	What did you really need?

Date Time	Trigger? What caused you to eat?	What food/ drink?	Thoughts? What were you thinking?	Feelings? How did you feel?	Hunger? How hungry? What type of hunger?	Consequences? Short term? Long Term?	What did you really need?

Food and Mood Journal

Date Time	Trigger? What caused you to eat?	What food/drink?	Thoughts? What were you thinking?	Feelings? How did you feel?	Hunger? How hungry? What type of hunger?	Consequences? Short term? Long Term?	What did you really need?

Date Time	Trigger? What caused you to eat?	What food/drink?	Thoughts? What were you thinking?	Feelings? How did you feel?	Hunger? How hungry? What type of hunger?	Consequences? Short term? Long Term?	What did you really need?

Food and Mood Journal

Date Time	Trigger? What caused you to eat?	What food/ drink?	Thoughts? What were you thinking?	Feelings? How did you feel?	Hunger? How hungry? What type of hunger?	Consequences? Short term? Long Term?	What did you really need?

Date Time	Trigger? What caused you to eat?	What food/ drink?	Thoughts? What were you thinking?	Feelings? How did you feel?	Hunger? How hungry? What type of hunger?	Consequences? Short term? Long Term?	What did you really need?

Food and Mood Journal

Date Time	Trigger? What caused you to eat?	What food/ drink?	Thoughts? What were you thinking?	Feelings? How did you feel?	Hunger? How hungry? What type of hunger?	Consequences? Short term? Long Term?	What did you really need?

Date Time	Trigger? What caused you to eat?	What food/ drink?	Thoughts? What were you thinking?	Feelings? How did you feel?	Hunger? How hungry? What type of hunger?	Consequences? Short term? Long Term?	What did you really need?

Food and Mood Journal

Date Time	Trigger? What caused you to eat?	What food/ drink?	Thoughts? What were you thinking?	Feelings? How did you feel?	Hunger? How hungry? What type of hunger?	Consequences? Short term? Long Term?	What did you really need?

Date Time	Trigger? What caused you to eat?	What food/ drink?	Thoughts? What were you thinking?	Feelings? How did you feel?	Hunger? How hungry? What type of hunger?	Consequences? Short term? Long Term?	What did you really need?

Food and Mood Journal

Date Time	Trigger? What caused you to eat?	What food/ drink?	Thoughts? What were you thinking?	Feelings? How did you feel?	Hunger? How hungry? What type of hunger?	Consequences? Short term? Long Term?	What did you really need?

Date Time	Trigger? What caused you to eat?	What food/ drink?	Thoughts? What were you thinking?	Feelings? How did you feel?	Hunger? How hungry? What type of hunger?	Consequences? Short term? Long Term?	What did you really need?

Food and Mood Journal

Date Time	Trigger? What caused you to eat?	What food/ drink?	Thoughts? What were you thinking?	Feelings? How did you feel?	Hunger? How hungry? What type of hunger?	Consequences? Short term? Long Term?	What did you really need?

Date Time	Trigger? What caused you to eat?	What food/ drink?	Thoughts? What were you thinking?	Feelings? How did you feel?	Hunger? How hungry? What type of hunger?	Consequences? Short term? Long Term?	What did you really need?

Food and Mood Journal

Date Time	Trigger? What caused you to eat?	What food/drink?	Thoughts? What were you thinking?	Feelings? How did you feel?	Hunger? How hungry? What type of hunger?	Consequences? Short term? Long Term?	What did you really need?

Date Time	Trigger? What caused you to eat?	What food/drink?	Thoughts? What were you thinking?	Feelings? How did you feel?	Hunger? How hungry? What type of hunger?	Consequences? Short term? Long Term?	What did you really need?

Food and Mood Journal

Date Time	Trigger? What caused you to eat?	What food/ drink?	Thoughts? What were you thinking?	Feelings? How did you feel?	Hunger? How hungry? What type of hunger?	Consequences? Short term? Long Term?	What did you really need?

Date Time	Trigger? What caused you to eat?	What food/ drink?	Thoughts? What were you thinking?	Feelings? How did you feel?	Hunger? How hungry? What type of hunger?	Consequences? Short term? Long Term?	What did you really need?

Congrats kings & queens

I am so excited for you! You have made the choice to take your life and your health seriously by committing to forming new healthy eating habits.

Following this six week plan will give you the jumpstart you need to achieve your health eating goals. I specifically designed this plan with eating options that you'll actually enjoy to make this program as easy as possible! I look forward to celebrating your results!

Don't forget to go to my website and check out my other books "Boundaries+Clarity=Peace", "The Diva Code", and "Diva's Don't Deflect They Journal".

🌐 mylifecoachtandy.com

📷 @lifecoachtandy

f @tandysaidit

✉ transform@mylifecoachtandy.com

Redesign Your Life